WE WHO HAVE GONE
BEFORE . . . .

WE WHO HAVE

GONE BEFORE

❖❖❖❖

Memory and an Old Wilderness Midwife

STEVEN FOSTER

THE SCHOOL OF LOST BORDERS

ILLUSTRATIONS

SELENE FOSTER

Lost Borders Press
P.O. Box 55
Big Pine, CA 93513
e-mail: lostbrdrs@telis.org
www.schooloflostborders.com

Library of Congress Cataloging-in-Publication Data

Foster, Steven, 1938—

We who have gone before: memory and an old wilderness midwife

cm.

ISBN 0-9667659-2-3 $19.75

1. Eco-psychology; 2. Psychology; 3. Psycho-Philosophy;
4. Autobiography in Nature

LCCN: Pending

CIP

Edited and designed by Sarah Felchlin
Front and back cover by Selene Foster: Acrylic, ink, and charcoal on paper, 2001.

First Edition
Manufactured in USA

At present the question is open. It is possible that we do, after all, live in an amnesiac world that is governed by eternal laws. But it is also possible that memory is inherent in nature; and if we find that we are indeed living in such a world, we shall have to change our way of thinking entirely. We shall sooner or later have to give up many of our old habits of thought and adopt new ones; habits that are better adapted to life in a world that is living in the presence of the past—and is also living in the presence of the future, and open to continuing creation.

—Rupert Sheldrake, *The Presence of the Past*

DEDICATION

This book was born in the protest movements of the early 1970s while I was teaching Modern Literature at San Francisco State University, when psychedelic love was transformed into revolutionary fervor by the Viet Nam war, the Black Power movement, and Wounded Knee. I could not resist the call for change. When advocates of a Black Studies Department appeared in my classroom one day, demanding to be heard, I dropped the agenda—Brecht's "Mother Courage"—and surrendered the podium. I can still remember the gist of what they said. "You cannot return to your former lives."

In the twinkling of an eye, the young professor changed his tune. The idea of revolution no longer seemed a literary idea. It was an historical inevitability. Heads were being bloodied every day on campus to keep a few classrooms open, and the FBI was watching my house because I was a suspected enemy of the state.

It was then that We Who Have Gone Before began to whisper in my ear. Of course they had been there from the moment I had been conceived, but I had never listened carefully to them. Now they would not let me rest. They kept telling me that fulfillment was not in analyzing literary works for their intellectual content. Fulfillment was not in resisting with booby traps and bombs and radical protests. Fulfillment lay in finding out for myself where my truth was hiding, and then doing something about it.

So I obeyed the ancient calling and forsook the quaking tower of ivory and went into the marketplace. I left everything I had so carefully built: wife, children, profession, comfortable life story. I rolled the dice. The times were so desperate I didn't even look to see what numbers came up. I assumed it was snake eyes and set out on the Yellow Brick Road.

I didn't pick up a gun. I went alone into the desert to ask what I could do for myself. The answer was clear. True revolution would never come about until the children remembered the way to get to adulthood—and the adults to true elderhood—and the elders to honorable death. And none of this would ever come to pass unless I learned the ancient art of birthing myself, and, by definition, others of my species, through rites of passage in wild nature, our true mother home.

I will never forget the day this revolutionary notion came into my head. I was in a company car crossing the Bay Bridge, San Francisco to Oakland/Berkeley. Cars whizzed past as I become lost in an epiphany: "I can do this!" I began to climb a mountain called We Who Have Gone Before. I will never reach the summit. At the age of eligibility for AARP and Alpah One Anti-trypsin genetic definiency, I am still climbing. As I hold to my current karmic purchase, trying to catch my breath, I see inscrutable trees, glittering rocks, and a mystical sky. It seems I will never be able to climb any higher.

My hopes exceed my faltering abilities. But I must go on. I must continue even when it appears that life work was in vain. The revolution has not come. And the culture has hardly raised a finger, except to become more protective of itself.

This book is many books condensed into thoughts, reflections, recollections, fermentations, meditations, feelings re-felt in tranquility. Admittedly, it is like a smorgasbord of *aperitifs*. Tempting, yes. But where is the main course?

The main course is the book itself. Surely one can fill oneself on appetizers. These *bon mots* may not slate the great hunger of the soul for the forgotten wisdom of our sacred forbears—an emptiness only the future can fill—but they may stimulate the appetite for restaurants offering main courses.

Apparently, I was always fated to struggle against seemingly insurmountable odds. No regrets. Sooner or later, most of us are reminded of the old ancestral adage: "It's not the goal but the journey that counts." As death approaches, I see that we must all carry on to the end, without self-pity, no matter what experiences the journey requires. I carry on, because, to tell the truth, I am too stubborn to let go. Deep in my soul I want to die well. And I am asking for your compassion.

Has my mountain climb brought me to completion? Of course not. I have just begun the ascent. I have just begun to breathe. I am nothing but a foetus, and I owe my impending birth to We Who Have Gone Before.

This book is dedicated to our Sacred Ancestors.

ILLUSTRATIONS

Two years after she had graduated from Bard College with a major in Art, I gave a rough version of this book to my daughter, Selene. She responded with designs she had created during her senior year.

Her own way of entering maturity is evident in the visual aspect of this book. In these designs you can trace the odyssey of her journey as a young artist transported from "Kansas" (Big Pine, CA) to the Yellow Brick Road. Because Selene is resourceful, loving, charismatic, beautiful, and endlessly inventive, she will reach many an Emerald City.

Walk with me through the wilderworld of Selene's artistic memory. Her name, "moon" in classical Greek, bespeaks her mythical ancestry. She was conceived on Ithaka, the home of Odysseus, the "wide-wanderer" of Homer's Odyssey. Still in her mother's womb, she narrowly escaped death in a freak accident at Phorky's Bay, where the mythical hero finally landed after 20 years at sea. This was the first passage of her own personal odyssey. She came within an instant of death. For some reason, the car hurtling toward us like a cartwheeling acrobat chose a slightly different vector as it thundered past with a glancing blow.

On the Great Ballcourt, Death appreciates those who dance well, and allows them to live again—for the benefit of the living. Apparently, we were dancing well enough.

I told Selene what I was looking for were roots and threads of living and dying things, shreds and shards of light in the deepest darkness of places beyond thought, aggregations of improbabilities, implausible relationships, evolutionary memories, abrupt self realizations, and insane mysteries. She gave me these prints and paintings. Judge for yourself. Her vision is truly hers—and her sacred ancestors'.

Some day the illustrations in this book will represent a phase in the development of a significant artistic genius. Please continue.

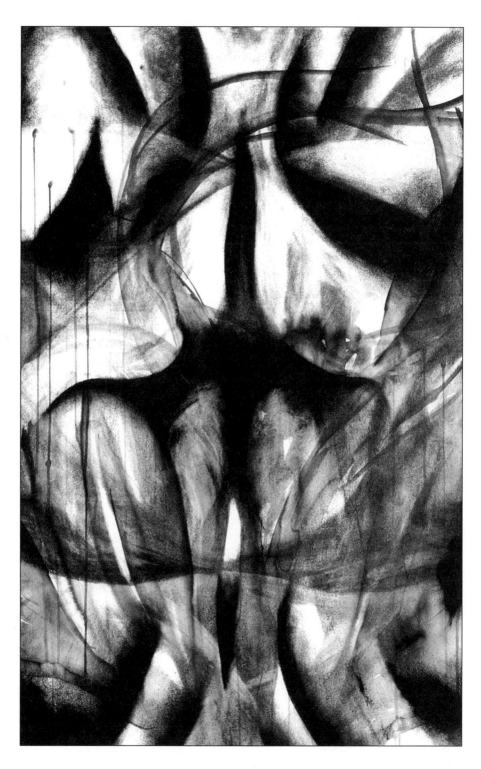

Selene Foster: Charcoal and ink on paper, '98

ACKNOWLEDGMENTS

Gratefully and with the deepest respect, I thank Norman Spinrad, spinner of magnificent allegories of our time, especially for his magnificent novel, *Child of Fortune*. He tells it like he sees it, and what he sees will come to pass, centuries from now—*if homo sapiens is fortunate enough to survive*.

As Spinrad envisions it, after great tribulations, we will reach many earths, many homes. Then a great cultural disintegration will come, for the children will not be growing into maturity. Because they have been given everything, they will have little interest in their destiny. At this juncture, the strange artifacts of We Who Have Gone Before will be found.

Among the old memories of those who went before is the secret of the "jump drive"—a means of instantaneously reaching light-years distant worlds. With this new (archaic) wisdom, will come a renaissance in the rites of passage of the young. Once again the children will leave home at the age of 18 and travel the universe on a "wander year," seeking their destiny. In the life moment of a year, they will prove themselves to be true adults. The human race will survive.

I must also thank my love, Meredith, who saw me in ways I could never describe—who allowed me the freedom—who even accepted the hardest kinds of drudgery, so that I could find time to write. Any written communication arising from this keyboard carries an automatic "we."

Not me—no, never "me" alone—but us. Us to the end!

And finally I want to thank Sarah, who imprinted this book on surfaces of electromagnetic crystal, in codes and inscriptions I could never begin to understand. She arrived out of the blue from a far away region where people live with monsters like gridlock, living cost, dying oak trees, and sushi bars. And she answered, "Yes, I will put your words into QuarkX-Press. And furthermore, I will do it as well as a performance by Madonna or Dylan."

Thank you, Sarah. As far as I'm concerned, by this you have confirmed the right to seek your fortune as your heart desires.

Selene Foster: Collage and mixed media on paper, '98

TABLE OF CONTENTS

WE WHO HAVE GONE BEFORE

This book is written at the end of a life. There is nothing in it that does not owe its existence to sixty-five years of memory. Not much when compared to the memory of the human race—but enough for me— enough because it is part and parcel of the whole.

When I went into the wilderness to fast alone, I was accompanied by memories. With such constant companions, how could I ever have been bored? At any given moment I lived with hundreds, no, thousands of ghosts in thousands of centuries, in thousands of scenarios I had already lived, or wish I had lived. If I couldn't remember exactly what happened, or with whom, it made little difference in the end. I remembered what I remembered.

Any life is worth the living, if only for the memories. The good ones. The bad ones. The lies. The dreams. The truths to grow on. I look around at my neighbors. They too are remembering because they cannot help but remember. We would not be alive if we were not remembering.

We have stitched our future together with these threads. As we pass through the various stages and transitions of life, our bodies, our psyches, our minds and spirits took the form of memories. Always we will walk in the shoes of memory—to remember, recollect, reminisce, retrospect, re- consider, review, distinguish, commemorate, revive, recapture, call back, re- evoke, conjure up, refresh, restock, repeat, evoke, prompt, repeat, pass in review, get by heart. . . And our death will be an event staged by memories.

I invite you to take a journey with We Who Have Gone Before.

Selene Foster: Mixed media on paper, '99

THE FOUR SHIELDS

Every winter, Meredith and I go down to the Death Valley wilderness with a few close friends to fast alone for four days and nights. We walk away from the vehicles, each in our own direction, and we don't see each other until we return. That we be allowed this time alone and apart is of utmost importance to us. How could we be midwives in wilderness rites of passage if the threshold experience were not always fresh in our own memories?

Memory unlocks the therapeutic cupboard. What the candidate brings back from the threshold is a story based entirely on remembered events. As such, it comprises an altered version of "the real." Can there be any doubt that what really happened and our memory of what happened are quite different? What is real and what is remembered are two distinct—yet related—realities. Indeed, could it be that memory is more "real" than what actually, physically, happened? What we remember is absolutely essential to our health, adaptability, survival, and growth into fullness.

Last winter, while fasting in Death Valley, I was aware, as never before, of the relationship between memory and the threshold "ordeal." As I left the others and hiked alone into the desert, I began to swim in a sea of memory. Inwardly, not a single idea, thought, image, feeling, emotion, or sensation arose that was not a part of my own memory field. And outwardly, not a single encounter, event, symbol, species, marked my travels that was not related to the memory of "nature." Personal memory, natural memory—how can we draw distinctions between person and nature? Borders are lost.

Define: "person," or "self." Does your definition rule out the "we memory" of the sacred ancestors, singing in our veins? Of course not. It's impossible.

We were remembering, and nature was remembering in us. Together we were remembering how to survive, grow, perpetuate, nurture, and evolve. We were remembering who we were and where we were going—remembering together as one—like God putting his human self back together. Like God regenerating.

Specifically, what did I remember? I remembered in my body. I lived with all the experiences I had accumulated from infancy—sensations, tensions, hungers, and needs. And I remembered the consequences of my deeds in the dark, rainbow chambers of my psyche, acts of omission and commission, recollections rich with conscience, insight and feeling. I remembered and was remembered in the eons-long dreams and day dreams of We Who Have Gone Before.

I remembered my place in the ecosystem, in the scheme of things, in the nurture and maintenance of my species within the cosmic, archival field in which my puny little local memory was a mote—but a necessary mote—in the unfolding design of immensity.

I would be walking along and something in the path would catch my eye—a stone, a plant, a stretch of dappled shade, a patch of sky, a bird song, the drone of a fly. Suddenly, without warning, I would be swimming in the sea of memory.

SEASON

The four seasons and the four directions exist because God keeps "remembering" nature. Nature exists because all the species have to keep remembering birth, death, copulation, interdependency, and all that behavior absolutely necessary to our existence as one.

Because we remember, we can collectively create our destiny. Our collective recollections have the power to alter all things.

When the candidate brings a story back from the wilderness threshold, we treat the memory as real. And what we mirror back to the story teller comes from our own memory banks. Memory mirrors memory, and from this fortuitous commingling future memories are born.

When I was a child I ran headlong through the changes of season with hardly a thought. Enthralled by the innocent energy of my body, I tried to live winter as summer, and fall as spring.

As I grew older, I had to change my tune. There were differences between the seasons. I couldn't live as if there were not. It would be folly. I had loved ones to care for. Part of caring for them meant I had to care for myself. Summer was one thing, winter was another.

It took a long time for me to finally realize that I had to store up for the winter by reaping, every fall, the summer growth I had sowed in the spring.

SUMMER

Summer is for children. No doubt we had many memorable summers as we grew older. Even in our dying days, we will often remember summer from the perspective of the child we are, and always will be—perhaps so even on the other side of death's gate.

The fact is, summer is a memory of earth. Because the earth keeps remembering to wobble on her axis, the seasons pass. Summer is one of the electromagnetic memories of Mother Earth.

Physics—the study of the physical world—is the science of the child's body. And never is that body more manifest than in the summer. Body, not soul. The soul of the child does not fully manifest itself until the fall. Until then, the child revels innocently in the body, often without conscience or thought. The days are long and hot. The nights are short and warm. School is out. The sun shines down "uncivilized" commands: Take off your clothes and be naked. Open your pores. Flex your muscles. Run, jump, crawl, fly, dive, swim, laugh, cry, sweat, be tense, angry and lustful, and above all, play.

When summer arrives, the insects come out in earnest. Mosquitoes, gnats, fleas, wasps, ants, bees, aphids—name your pet peeve. Most of the time we don't really want to look at that incredible universe that hovers and slithers across our vulnerable skin: creepy crawlies of sting and bite and bother. Get off me, we snarl, and fortify ourselves with unguents, oils, and repellents. We fight an evasive action, outnumbered a billion to one.

I learned a valuable lesson one summer. I was fasting in the mountains of Death Valley and a huge cactus fly kept trying to crawl into my nose. If my nose had been smaller, I might not have been so bothered. But this fly seemed to think the vasty interior of my nose was a mansion of worship. Consequently, I whacked the rascal so hard that I bloodied my nose. The fly fell to the ground, seemingly dead. Ha! I smugged. Serves you right, you big galoot.

Immediately, a red ant appeared, and began to circle the stunned fly in tighter and tighter loops, until it zeroed in on its prey and stung it. The fly quivered. The ant stung again. The fly groveled, looking for a leg hold so it could spread its wings and escape. "No way," gritted the ant. In a killing frenzy, it stung the fly again, and again, until the desperate creature gave a mighty heave and actually spread its wings. Too late. Twenty ants had arrived, as if by magic, to attach themselves to the fly. It shuddered and rolled over, legs kicking in the air. The fight was over. The irritating but innocent fly became the prize of the red ants, who carried it off triumphantly to the feast of their sacred hill.

I felt sick to my stomach. I was well aware of the old vision quest adage not to harm any living creature, not even a fly. But in the summer, the violence of nature prevails. If everything young and growing is trying to survive, then it simply makes sense that there is bound to be some competition for living space. Invariably there will be casualties.

In the summer, there is no morality, no "love your neighbor like yourself." There is only "love yourself." Without conscience, and behaving perfectly in accord with natural instincts, species will murder other species just to stay alive.

Memorializing summer, Annie Dillard said, "We sleep with a mouthful of blood." How did we get blood in our mouths? By killing and eating, by laying waste to life around us, by innocently, instinctually doing our best to stay alive. We mustn't fool ourselves. We are no different from our brothers and sisters. Blood tastes good to us. Without it we would not be alive. The memory screams inside us. "Bring me more blood!"

I'm not just talking to those who are meat eaters. We all share in the summer's "survival of the fittest" memory. We know, because we remember what we must do. Sometimes it's a flinch; sometimes it's a slap; sometimes it's a systematic plan of genocide against bugs, weeds, parasites— threats real or imaginary.

Why, just the other day we captured two house mice who were laying waste to the food in our cupboards. I transported them to a nearby field, rationalizing to myself that at least I wasn't killing them. But I knew down deep inside that they were house mice. They didn't stand a chance out here in the unfamiliar fields with the red-taileds by day and the great horneds by night.

Summer. I wonder exactly how it will feel when Mother Nature circles in and stings me repeatedly—until I become ant food.

In the summer, we take our people high into the mountains. It would be folly to stay down low, where ambient temperatures hover around 100. In the mountains, the sun burn factor is higher, but the days and nights are cooler. The shade of a juniper or a pinyon can be downright chilly.

There are drawbacks, however, to higher altitudes. Up there, we are vulnerable to one of summer's oldest memories—lightning storms.

I am no expert in weather patterns. There are times when sudden aberrations in climate completely mystify me—like the day it snowed on the 4th of July. Thunderstorms, on the other hand, are quite predictable. They arrive every year, just as the summer is getting intolerably hot, almost always in the months of July and August. And let me tell you, a lightning storm in the Inyo-White Range is something to behold.

We tell people to get down off the ridges. Don't shelter under lone trees. Stay away from large boulders. Don't stand up. Grovel. That's what we tell them. Grovel.

And, when the storm arrives, pray.

I find myself groping for an analogy to summer lightning storms, something that will explain why they should exist. If weather is a kind of earth-memory—and it is—then these storms are reenactments of what humans call trauma, memories sucked into vortexes and thermals, lurid agitations of psychological heat and air, clashings and thrashings and flailings of feeling, when calmness and serenity are ripped open by primeval forces erupting from a four billion year past, when life first appeared on earth.

No doubt these lightning-memories can be death-dealing. They are also life-enhancing. In the summer, earth remembers to be violent, to infuse inert proteins with the electric magic of life, to ignite, inflame, boil and burn, to ravage the face of calm, and to penetrate the darkness of deep, where life stirs and dreams.

"Why?" I scream at the sudden fury of wind, the glower of clouds, the abysmal sink in the pit of my stomach. All at once my view of the broad landscape of life has been forced to a single perspective, and I am looking at the blade of the Reaper. "Have you no heart?" I cry at the blinding, silent tongues.

But I know deep inside that the lightning is remembering to enact itself in the cosmic masquerade. And because I am also a player in the masquerade, I too must remember—with the ages-long fear of We Who Have Gone Before.

Summer always brings mosquitoes. As the water warms, so does nature's lust for blood. Out here where we live at the edge of the desert, the scourge appears in the late spring. God knows where they come from. The mosquito abatement man comes around to assure us he is taking care of the problem in our immediate area. But we have learned to distrust the promise in his voice. His primary job seems to have little to do with actually controlling the epidemic. He's just a public relations man.

We employ all kinds of organic tricks to control the pests. We keep the water flowing swiftly in our creek. We float baptimos briquets in our lake. We install bat houses in the trees. We breed trout. We take samples of the water from our land, looking for telltale larvae. No matter. The little bloodsuckers come and go as they please.

By mid-June we realize that there is nothing we can do. We simply have to live with them, and, no matter how grudgingly or how often we slaver on repellent, offer up our blood.

Summer is the time of bloodletting. Summer requires that along with all the other mammals, we give of our bodies so that the bloodsuckers may live. Actually, we have to account ourselves fortunate. What about those martyrs in the gulags of Siberia who were tied naked to stakes for days on end so that they could feed vast hordes of mosquitoes and gnats? Those who survived never lived very long. One mosquito takes a nip. Millions drink quarts.

There have been times when I tried to reason with the memory of Mother Nature. Why? Why? Why do you remember to breed all these blood suckers?

She always answers: "Life." And she always remembers to put a tick in the woodpile.

FALL

Everybody talks about it. There is a difference in the air. All at once the sprawling heat of summer is tempered by a constrictive force. Cooler? Yes, but the temperature may in fact go down only infinitesimally. It's something else, something more akin to the realization that childhood is finished, innocence is over, playtime is past, eternity has come to a close.

No doubt, change is a law of the universe. Nothing stays the same. Our naive bodies may choose to turn away, but We Who Have Gone Before know all too well that if we seek eternity, the only way is to embrace change.

And so when fall comes, we know it right away. There is an ancient bitter-sweetness to the air, a tang in the soul. We begin to remember other falls, other endings. We begin to think about the size of our woodpile, the adequacy of our diet. Like a mouse venturing out of its hole, a chill creeps into our veins.

There is no mystery to this. Because we are of nature, we remember what nature remembers. Nature remembers death just as often as she remembers birth.

I used to love the fall. Now something in me is afraid. That something is the vulnerability I feel because my days are numbered. There is nothing new about these feelings. Rationally, I know I'm not alone. Nevertheless, I experience the coming of fall as if I were the only one truly aware of what it means—that the leaves should shrivel and turn color and the fruit fall to the ground.

This extreme form of fall-subjectivity is undoubtedly connected to certain long-term memories of dying and we can't get them out of our systems—which is not to say that we feel the least bit morbid about dying. Even as our hearts sink in nameless dread, we can't help but notice the beauty falling around us. Surely, nothing is so poignant as the changing leaves of the aspen or the willow. When I see these heartbreaking colors appear, I know and love my earthly home, this life, this wonder, this hope.

When Adam and Eve were forced to leave the garden because God decided there should be seasons, they must have experienced the same perplexity. Adam turned to Eve and said, "Honey, I don't want to leave this place." And Eve must have replied, "Don't worry. We're just going away for a little while."

Eve was right. Every fall we have to leave this paradise again.

❖❖❖❖

A young man comes to see us. He calls himself "Crow." He's a product of the gangs of Los Angeles, although he has outgrown his frivolous youth. He has other things to think about—like the fact that he has a rare genetic disease called Marfan's Syndrome, which causes his body, including his organs, to grow unchecked and at different rates of speed. The doctors tell him he shouldn't be alive today. Yet he is, although he is very angry at the circumstances of his life. And because he is poor, he cannot obtain the medical help he needs.

Some time ago he came to grips with the reality of his predicament. Now he lives a life in which he wonders every day if the end has come. We are impressed by his intelligence, his insight, his artistic sensibilities. He is one of those warriors who learned the hard but necessary lesson that death is an ally. He reminds us of the reality of the fall passage. Sooner or later, we all undertake it. I am no different than Crow. You are no different than me. We will all wake up one day to discover that the leaves have shrivelled on the trees. There is no turning back.

I ask him if he wants more time. He says he's not sure he has the right to ask for it. He's being fatalistic—and more than a little ashamed. What's the difference between dying today and dying a few years from now? He says no difference, but I know that he would really rather live a little longer.

Crow and the rest of us dwell in Indian Summer. The leaves turn, but the weather stays warm. We tell ourselves that winter will come when it is ready. We wake up in the morning and look ahead to another day. But the unpicked apples are rotting on the limb. The north wind roars. The seed will fall into the frozen ground. Dead white, the color of all color, will blanket everything.

Please don't think I'm merely writing about Crow. I'm writing about We Who Have Gone Before.

Fall is the medium in which the soul flourishes best. And the approach of winter is the sunlight toward which the branches of the soul reach. When deep, dark clouds obscure the stars, and the wind freezes our breath, and the sky rains down barbs of sleet, and we are all alone, far beyond the comforts of home, our soul dreams of spring.

The coming of fall is not the end. We can wail and carry on about the poignancy of summer's end, but winter lies ahead. Not until the snowfall lies for days upon the ground are we ready to mourn the dying.

Remember last winter? Fall is not the end. If it were, we wouldn't be here, once again feeling the nostalgic pangs of fall.

The zero of the year is dead ahead. We would be blithering idiots to forget it.

WINTER

Winter doesn't just disappear at the spring equinox. Lord, no. You can celebrate the hell out of the equinox, and I hope it makes you feel better. You can gyrate, give your body away, act the perfect fool. But winter doesn't go away. Winter likes to grab spring in a dark alley and hold her down and have his way with her. She kicks and screams, which only makes it worse for us.

A late winter can devour the blossoms of the cherry and apricot trees. In one night, the fruit is gone. Leaves might still remain. Barren and forgotten, they rustle and look pretty as summer passes. You water and fertilize in the hope they will work up enough juice to last another year.

You think spring is so important? Maybe, but don't fool yourself. Winter always remembers what it has to do, and accomplishes its task with great self-importance. Like tonight, for example. In the middle of April, winter came down from the great northern mountains with gale force winds and smothering white.

Driving up the valley from Lone Pine in the frigid darkness, a sudden gust tore the driver's side wiper from the wind shield. Then, for good measure, it plastered the glass with heavy, wet snow. Cars coming the other way roared past only a few feet away, but we hardly saw them. Vision limited to a tiny hole I kept wiping clear in the left corner of the shield, I started to resentfully mutter that we were just trying to get home.

Home. Where the heart of spring lies incipiently in the woodpile beside the cold stove.

Winter never forgets its evolutionary mission—to delay, inhibit, wound, and suppress the spring—and to keep on ravishing until spring, like a young maiden who keeps her virginity through a gang rape, struggles up and, in the thunderous voice of summer, screams: "Enough is enough!"

I hate to be cold. Winter takes my breath away. It makes me struggle to live. I have to overcome the pain to survive. I dream of taking my ease in Baja, California. Of course, past age 60, I have learned that it doesn't matter in which latitude I live. Some variant of winter will come my way.

Only those initiated into the mysteries of earth's seasonal memories will understand what I mean. Winter exists equally on the equator or the poles.

Winter is simply Mother Earth's way of remembering to put that precious backbone into life to insure its survival—a strength not won without constant struggle.

Winter is a way of wishing it were not so, so that spring can be. We Who Have Gone Before remind us that if winter does not make us strong, we will not survive.

I love my woman. One of my deepest hopes is that she will live for many winters after I am gone. I write poetry to her while we are fasting alone, apart. I leave them at the stone pile.

I once told her (in a poem) that if I should happen to see her during those four days of fasting, my knees would lose their feet; I would fall, gash my wrists on sharp stones, and joyously bleed.

But words are nothing compared to what I feel. Winter has this quality. And poetry is a damn good way to get out of jail.

I just spent a couple of satisfying days in Death Valley with my son, his wife, and my granddaughter. Keenan and Patricia are insightful, mature parents. Olivia is strong, intelligent, and intuitive. Her talent is raw, egotistical, sometimes almost too much to handle. Olivia reminds me of what it really means to be a child with gifts and a growing inner sense of who she is.

But she would not be such a striking young woman if it were not for parental love. And believe me, this love is not easy to come by. It comes from remembering, profoundly, that winter will come. Children evoke this memory.

Parents and grandparents remember.

Spring is here. You'd hardly know it. You think you're only seeing winter. But actually you're seeing double. Though winter appears to rule in spades, you're holding a royal flush. Even as the north wind tears the petals away, the trees are blossoming.

SPRING

The coming of spring is joyous—and scary. Who knows what lies ahead? In the old days people celebrated the arrival of spring with the most outrageous behavior. They broke all the sacred rules of marriage, civic responsibility, and personal decorum. They spat in face of god, peed on their kings and magistrates, flashed their breasts and genitals in the most obscene manner. But nobody got busted. It was all okay. Because everybody did it, everybody forgave each other—even husbands and wives. Why? Because spring had come. Life had been reborn. And summer was on its way.

But there was a deeper reason why. Once you have been through a hard winter, you go a little crazy in spring. Carpe diem! There won't be too many more. Let it all hang out! It's all hanging out anyway.

The Trickster has always been associated with the coming of spring. Coyote and his kin remind us that spring goes crazy. Here in the Owens Valley, the Paiutes have a myth about how the world was created.

They say Coyote was floating around in a bullrush boat with Wolf, his father. And since there was nothing but water, Coyote got bored. He told Wolf he was sick and tired of doing nothing, and Wolf told him to pick up a rattle lying in the bottom of the boat. "Rattle," he said. "And don't stop rattling until you can't feel your arm."

So Coyote rattled. Night came on. And Coyote was just so antsy he rattled all through the night. When morning came he saw what had happened. There had been a hole in the rattle. All night, the seeds and soil and stuff had leaked out through the hole. An island had formed, big enough to moor the boat to.

Coyote got out, ran around the island a hundred times. Then he stopped and panted, "Wolf! It's not enough!"

They got back in the boat and Coyote started rattling again. He rattled all through the night and in the morning the Owens Valley lay before their eyes. Not the mountains, just the valley. Coyote got out of the boat and ran around for a long time, up and down the great valley, sniffing around. Finally, he came back to Wolf and panted, "Wolf. It's not enough."

By then Wolf was getting a little antsy himself. "Get back in the boat, you slat-sided bundle of hunger!" he ordered. "Rattle!"

So all night Coyote rattled, and in the morning the great mountain ranges, the Sierra Nevada and the Inyo-White reared their snowy crowns on both sides of the valley. Coyote's eyes bulged out of his head. All around him, the most beautiful and majestic region on earth! He ran and ran and ran to his heart's content. He ran to the tops of the Sierra. He ran to the tops of the Inyo-Whites. It took him days, weeks, months, years, to cover all the ground. Finally, he returned, tired as a dog, his tongue lolling out. "Wolf," he said. . . .

Many would call Coyote a fool. But the truth is, "not enough" is the birth-memory of spring. Enough has never been enough. And that's why it has arrived, birthed by the earth's memory to have more. Coyote comes up to us, tongue lolling.

"Woof!" he says. "It's not enough!"

Don't you tell me you know all about spring. I won't believe you. Not even gods or goddesses know what's going on. They just fuck all the way into summer, gestating mysteries.

It's an urge, an ancient urge, remembered in the body, psyche, mind, and spirit of the universe. I must have intercourse. I must copulate with what is because I want more.

Why?

You tell me why we have to have more. Isn't what has been given enough? "Enough! Or too much!" (Blake)

Tomorrow we put a group of trainees out on a March fast in the Eureka Valley. Horse Thief Canyon. The weather has not been good. Who knows what the next five days will bring? Probably fire and ice.

The first group in the spring always risks their lives a little bit more than the others. Spring can bring a fearsome disruption. I remember a time in the Reese River wilderness of Nevada when our group of teenagers was hit by a blinding blizzard in late June. Surprised by the storm, which crept in at dusk, we listened all night to the wailing of a girl who had been sequestered on solo nearby. In the morning we went to her aid. "I was cold and lonely," she said, ashamed that we had heard her cries.

Sometimes, glorious spring comes disguised as a blizzard. All night we cry from loneliness and self-pity, and nobody comes.

Spring always remembers to bring its shadow. From the place where the sun is brightest in the east, the deepest shadows are cast toward the west, where the sun goes down.

Selene Foster: Mixed media on paper, '99

Liminal Space and Memory

When the initiate crosses the threshold of the sacred wilderness world, he/she enters a morphogenetic field composed of hundreds, yea thousands, of discrete "morphogenetic fields." All these fields are interconnected, imbued with the memory of their "sacred ancestors," and compose the larger unity anthropologists call "liminal space." This space, governed by laws of time quite at variance with human conceptions, is constantly in the process of remembering itself, directing itself, preserving itself, evolving itself into a chaotic coherency that will persist and survive.

The human psyche in liminal space is also a morphogenetic field, discrete, yet connected to its own species, distinct yet subsumed, an inseparable part of all the other morphogenetic fields.

What happens when we enter liminal space? Though I cannot know for sure, I always have this spooky feeling that something is happening between me and all the species within my environment. I become aware of them (and they of me) and of all the ways in which we have remembered ourselves into existence. It's a kind of resonance, like a gong reverberating a full minute after it has been struck. I feel this resonance whenever I consciously interact with a particular field.

For example, if I find myself within a living clump of willow memory, and give my attention to "willow," a kind of electro chemical-magnetic resonance develops between me and willow—physical contacts, feelings of sensing and being sensed, inner images of "willow-ness," mental ideations of natural law involving willow as figure (the willow itself) and ground (willow as part of a larger whole), and spontaneous, artistic notions and memories of spirit and essence.

Morphogenetic resonance typifies liminal space.

I'm groping for the precise connection, the specific wavelength, on which willow and I can remember. I'm very curious about that. I would like to know exactly which memories willow is likely to evoke in the human memory field. These human memories, resonating to "willow memories," comprise a sub-field, a complex, and a window through which I can see myself and, with the help of We Who Have Gone Before, read the secrets of death and regeneration.

Space bulges with memories. Everything in the universe is remembering how to be itself and to play its part in the great cosmic drama. You walk into space and you walk into yesterday, into the past, into what was—and because it was—is. The past doesn't just disappear. It is transformed into memories. Memories accumulate. Not a jot or tittle is lost. The memories occupy space and overflow into time. They persist until they become actions, reactions, sensations, feelings, thoughts, dreams—until they compose a part of the mind of the Universal Morphogenetic Field.

The act of creation was an act of memory. God remembered that it was so. And, lo! It was.

There is no end to the remembering of God. Whenever God dies, he/she remembers to be born again—in liminal space.

❖❖❖❖

"Memories exist in space and continue in time. They are concentrated within and around the organisms they occupy. They are as much a part of life as breath. The function of memory is to organize habitual patterns of existence and the behavior of living things. Without memory (both inner and environmental) everything would die. And when living things die, memory doesn't. Memory lives on, and mediates between organisms and the whole by establishing 'rhythmic patterns of activity' that insure the continuance of life."

—Sheldrake, *The Presence of the Past*

We owe our memories to our ancestors as much as to our lives in the here and now. Because of my father's father's father, and the great expanses of the American west in which they lived, I have always been interested in geology, in the composition of minerals in rock, and the slow processes of transformation over eons of time. This interest became concentrated in the geologic strata of humans. Of what are we composed, and how, under the influences of environment and heredity, do we complete ourselves in this life?

Memory holds the clue. Because it is actually a substantial thing, as real as the atmosphere, we can study its composition, function, and laws. We can study memory fields and the ways they interact and change. Here are a few tantalizing clues. As my forefathers went through the rapid changes of the industrial revolution and the 20th century, their interest in earth geology (mitigated by ever-dwindling open spaces) evolved, in me, into human geology. Now I peel off layers of the psyche to get to the ancient core, the essential myths of human nature memory.

I see the same activity at work in my own children.

"Think of the past as pressed up, as it were, against the present, and as potentially present everywhere."

—Sheldrake, *The Presence of the Past*

For instance, our dog. Though I never knew her sire and dam, I can see them in her at any moment. They are evoked in her through her genetic breeding and by her interactions with the memory fields of her environment. At any given time, I can see the past as present everywhere she sniffs, touches, eats, hears, sees, and jumps.

We recently returned to a little village on the Greek island of Ithaka. Twenty-five years ago, while we were still falling in love, M and I had lived there for nine months, in a two-storey Greek shell of a house without electricity or plumbing or heating while we wrote a book together and succeeded in getting M pregnant with our daughter, Selene.

Oddly enough, the people of the village remembered us. They even had a photo of us (attending a baptism) in one of the tavernas. Most of our old friends were already dead. Nevertheless, the memory of our stay had clung to the harbor, and when the news came out that we had returned, villagers came from everywhere to welcome us back.

What had happened to our house in the meantime? After we left, it stood vacant for many years. Then it was rented out to a refugee couple from Albania, who lived there for two years. Then a man from England, wife deceased, lived there alone for many years, until he disappeared. Nobody knew where. Finally, a man from the National Theater of Greece found it on a vacation one day, and decided to buy it, to fix it up, to install plumbing and electricity, to paint the rooms and create a kitchen and bathroom.

The man, Dimitreus, invited us in. The old house had been transformed. But the old bare walls, so beautifully painted over, knew us. The memories we had left behind knew us. Immediately they knew us.

How did we know that we had been remembered? Some memories you wonder, maybe. But some memories are so strong you cannot divide them from such false distinctions as "inner" or "outward." Our memories knew us. There could be no mistake.

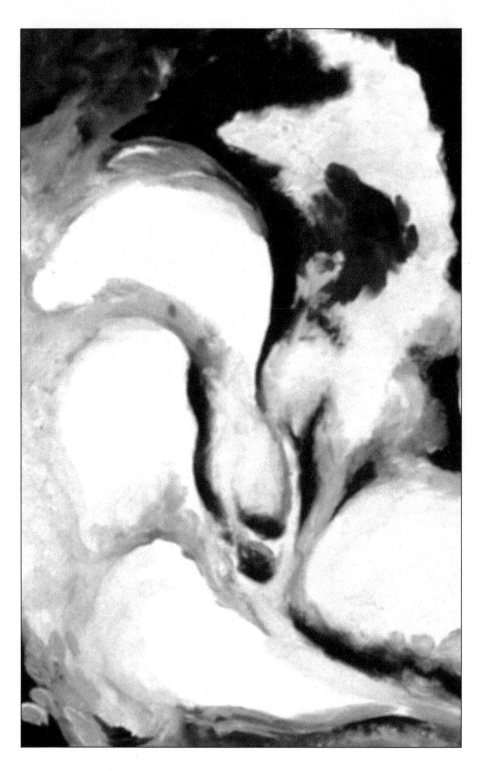

Selene Foster: Oil on wood, '01

SOUL AND DREAMING

It matters to people what happens to their souls—while they are living and after they die. The word crops up everywhere. It is used to sell everything, from perfume to religion. Certain things or sensations or feelings are said to "satisfy to the soul." There is soul this and soul that and "music to soothe the soul." Billie Holiday sings: "I'd give my soul just to call you my own." People everywhere look for a "soul mate." But nowhere is the word more current than in churches and synagogues. God or Jesus, loves the soul and "saves" it. By believing in certain ideas, our souls are "sanctified." There are good souls and bad souls. The good souls go to Paradise, the bad souls go to Hell.

Soul seems to have come from the idea of movement. The word itself comes from Old English (*sawol*) via the original Greek word, *Aiolos*, hence *saiwolos*, which literally means "quick-moving," or "easily moved." Soul seems to hinge on the idea of fleetingness or precariousness. The soul is quick because it can be easily moved from within or by an outside force.

I want to nail this definition down, now that I face the fear of dying every day. "Spirit" I can understand easily enough. Because my lungs are the cause of my distress, I can locate spirit in my breathing. As long as I can breathe in and out, I am spirit. When I cease to breathe in and out, spirit goes elsewhere.

But soul? If soul is that within me which moves quickly, then what exactly is moving? Life itself? Certainly. But life is too broad a definition. Soul has something to do with being alive—perhaps a quality or condition of life. Many times I have decided to sit very still, to feel what it was in me that was moving so fast. Beneath the breathing, beneath the gurgling of the plumbing, beneath the hum of muscles and nerves and the surging of blood and the symphony of chemicals, something was indeed moving very quickly. The more I tuned into that movement, the more I saw that soul is not strictly physical. For reasons I am still learning to understand, I have chosen to call that movement psychical, as opposed to physical.

The other day I was grubbing around in the garden. I had just planted some turnips and the spring sun was pulsing down little finger touches and I was feeling supremely happy. So I just sat there in the dirt and let all my burdens go. Physically, I was at rest. But something else was going on inside me which was not at rest. I would call it mind, but it had little to do with thought. It was a quicksilvery movement, more like feeling than thought, and it had much less to do with where I was in space and time. My eyes were open, looking down at the soil. A worm was sliding through a pile of overturned dirt. But I was only peripherally aware of the worm.

I was remembering, in bits and flashes, events, people, places, situations. For no apparent or immediate reason these particular memories were thronging consciousness, pulling me here and there like a leaf in a whirlwind. In a very real sense, the worm was pulling me through the dirt of feeling. Without conscious resistance, I was allowing myself to go wherever We Who Have Gone Before took me.

The closer I get to death, the more I am aware of my soul. I think my soul is who I am because of the sum total of my past memories. In the end, it doesn't matter whether these memories are true or false—although many of them are as factual as a stretch of road or a building entered or lived in. What matters is the split second when the memory comes into consciousness. This instant is an eternity. Linked to scores of other instants, it comprises a kind of contact with what is enduring. By "enduring" I mean what will be of use to me when I die.

Once, when I went to the desert to fast, it was early spring in the Confidence Hills of Death Valley. The second day, the wind stalked me like a tiger. As the day wore on, the storm increased until I could not stand against it. Dust arose from the sands, filling my mouth with alkali. Gradually, I began to experience the deepest fears. My lungs, already weakened by a genetic disease that was slowly killing me, shrank in terror.

I did what I could do. I crawled into my sleeping bag and squeezed up against the creosote bush that had been my shelter and my home, tailfirst into the dust. I made a tiny breathe hole, no larger than an egg, in my bag. I lay in that bag for hours as the wind twisted me like a leaf.

But the branches of the creosote anchored me to breath. After a while, I realized with a certain notion I can only attribute to We Who Have Gone Before, that I would pass through this ordeal. I would survive because "our souls" were breathing for me. In-out, in-out, in-out. My chest was rising and falling, steadily, surely, firmly, unaffected by the violence breaking loose around me. Without consciously intending, I had worked my way into a safe harbor, secured my lungs to a buoy, and, though the ropes were straining—they would hold me fast.

The wind died at nightfall. The dust settled back into itself. Stiff and sore, I crawled from the bag and sat cross-legged, looking up at the darkening sky. The crescent moon was falling westward, lured by voluptuous Venus. Softly, in gusts, the winds emptied their lungs and fell silent. Silence. Dark indigo suffused the sky over the southern Panamints. Overhead, stars appeared, more eternal than diamonds.

Dead calm and clear.

It was then I saw my end. First will come the wind to fill my lungs with particles of death. There will be no way to avoid this insinuation. Twist and thrash as I will, my breath will take my soul through. In-out, in-out—*in . . . . out . . . .*

Then there will be a great calm. Everything will become crystal clear. *. . . In. . . . Out.*

We Who Have Gone Before teach us about dying. In the great storm they will come to our distress calls. Our souls will go with us through the thunder to the paradise on the other side, where we all become one.

The terms memory and soul are nearly synonymous. By soul I refer to that inner self, that special inner self—somehow a piece of the greater Self—that is the sum total of its memories.

My soul is a striving to remember who I am, to make who I am compatible with who I was born to be, to bring who I am into synch with who I will be. My soul is a temporal striving to fill the space of my body, a sense of self that clings to space so that it can complete itself in time.

Eros is the soul remembering to germinate and sprout, so that life will continue. Eros is the song of the soul. And through that song, in contrapuntal rhythm, runs another memory—death—the death-memory of We Who Have Gone Before.

When I go to sleep, I sleep. Now and then a dream comes—occasionally a very powerful one. Why the dream comes then, and not some other time, is often a mystery to me. I keep hoping that the fact I am nearing death will bring particularly powerful dreams. There are indications that this may be so. Nevertheless, I have always been respectful of those who have rich dream lives.

What is the connection between dreams and memory? I'm not sure there is any difference. Dreams seem to be just another form of memory—ancestral memory, if you will (and here I must bow in the direction of Jung). And if dreams are memory, they also occur in the past, present, and future—simultaneously. If they have any remarkable characteristic, it is the fact that they exist in linear time.

Memories also exist in non-linear time. And like dreams, they "lie." That is, the fact that you dream it, or remember it, does not necessarily make it true of your waking consciousness. But the "lie" can also be truer than truth, and the time/space resonance includes not only the past and present, but the future.

I am tempted by the word "imagination." I wonder what the difference is between dream, memory, and imagination. Not much, I think. Dreaming is a way of remembering. Re-membering is a way of "image-ing"—imagining as our ancestors imaged it.

I find it quite easy to "image" the past in such a way as to alter my future. I can remember so imaginatively that I crave (or avoid) certain future actions. In this I am no different than all the other species. I can certainly see dreaming as simply another way of remembering the past in order to alter the future. Or, just as validly, another way of remembering the future in order to alter the past.

I had a prescient dream one night while I was fasting in the Eureka Valley. I was in a cluttered house. Outside the windows, flames were roaring like a thunderstorm. The house was burning down. Powerless to quench the fire, or to escape, I curled up on an unkempt bed, watching a horribly misshapen creature approach, apparently with the intention of lying down with me. Filled with loathing, I tried to ward the thing from my bed. But the creature would not be restrained. I was afraid it wanted to have intercourse.

Selene Foster: Charcoal on paper, '98

The house was burning down. I remembered that I was dreaming. I was that frightened man lying on that filthy bed, and I had to take charge of the situation before it really got out of hand.

I let the horrible thing approach. I don't know why. It was a dream. Slobbering tears of gratefulness, it lay down beside me. The fire outside the window howled and thundered. I put my arm around its shoulder. Flesh came off in my fingers, like jelly.

The creature did not want to make love with me. It wanted to lie in my arms and be grateful.

The dream ended in the here and now. We were safe for the moment, the beast and I, lying in each other's arms.

Within a year I was diagnosed with a fatal, genetic lung disease [alpha 1 antitrypsin deficiency]. My cluttered body was burning down around my ears and I was lying in bed with monstrous, misshapen lungs. I realized that for much of my life I had been unconsciously self-destructive, wooing the disease, even while I was trying to distance myself from it.

Like the dream said, I would either have to accept the monster karma, and live with it, or be consumed by the fires of mortality.

Was it the dream? Was it my imagination? What was it that assessed my past in terms of the present and saw into the future? Was it We Who Have Gone Before?

The earth dreams. She heaves like a giantess, dreaming of four billion years of life, copulation, and death. After all those years, I have begun to remember what she remembers as she sleeps in her cradle of infinite stars.

What does the earth dream? What memories does she maintain and nurture?

The earth is dreaming in four universal dimensions. First of all, she is dreaming of her body—or should I say, she is "re-membering" her body—re-membering all her parts, re-membering their creation, and re-membering how, where, and when these parts are birthing or dying. She is re-membering her pleasure in her body, and all the ways in which she physically reenacts love.

The second dream comes from her soul. By soul I mean her awareness of re-membering. Let the scientists rage at the truth, and waste thousands of years trying to disprove her soul. The truth seems obvious. She re-members what has happened to her, and she knows what she has to do to continue, though her course leads her through a billion years of nothingness. Her remembrance of life will prevail. There is nothing humans can do to alter that kind of memory-destiny. My soul rejoices with her. Her assured survival means that I will survive too. My soul is her soul.

Her third dream is of obedience—control in chaos, harmony in disintegration. She re-members light and darkness, substance and nothingness. She re-members every Law her recollecting has established: laws of balance and exchange, of singularity and interrelatedness, of conservation and mutability, of metaphor and process.

Her fourth dream is too beautiful for words. In this dream she sings, and in her songs are recorded every one of the secrets of birth, and her refusal to *ever* die.

If the earth is dreaming, she is also, and always, re-singing through her voice, re-membering the songs of spring, the songs of her own beginning, the songs about the impossible leap of the spark of nothingness for the tinder.

The New Age has come up with something called "lucid dreaming." Dream gurus conduct workshops in which people learn how to awaken from their dreams and control the plot. I'm fascinated by this agenda. The dream teachers seem to be trying to get people to do what the earth is always doing. Why shouldn't we learn to do what the earth does?

There is a magic key here for anyone who cares to pick it up. The key fits the lock on a door marked Very Big Secret, and it opens into wonder. The idea that the earth—and humans by relation—are in league with the dream—is quite awesome.

"Lucid dreaming" opens the door to the realization that we can control our dream of death. Not by "belief in heaven," but by assurance that we have a say about what happens after we die—that all we have to do is rise up in this helpless dream we are having about ourselves and take control of the outcome.

Better said than done? Maybe not.

MYTH: TRUTH AND LIES

Far be it from us to say what is true or false. Still, we have a lot of notions about T/F, and act on them all the time.

"True?" What do we mean by "true?" And what do we mean by "false?"

How true are our dreams and how false is the evidence of our senses? Primitive cultures consider the dream to be as real as the evidence of the senses.

Does "true" always equal "real?" I hope not. Truth seems deeper than the physical. Truth often requires a quieter assent, a "yes" from the core of our being. *Yes*. That is how life goes. *Yes*. I remember—if only because my own memory is the collective memory of my sacred ancestors. *Yes*. I remember the Truth. *Yes*. Even when I am simply daydreaming, I am remembering with *We*.

Let's go back to childhood. Try to remember the "truth" in terms of what actually happened. If our parents are still alive and if we have brothers and sisters, we can compare the truth of our memories with theirs. And I am often disappointed to find that the memories of others who were there at the time do not coincide with my own. Here I'd been living all those years thinking thus and so happened, and then someone else comes along and says: "I was there too, and I don't remember it happening that way." In this sense, the "truth"—i.e., what actually happened—seems to depend on the rememberer.

Historical truth is therefore suspect. It is subjective to the one who remembers. And "subjective truth"—such as the dream—is also suspect. We don't really trust the reality of our dreams. Sometimes they seem so unconnected to the nitty gritty bedrock of daily life.

The same for the memory of the time my mother slapped me. She didn't slap me, she says. And my brother, who was there, says she merely became angry with me. My memory of the slap serves me false.

Or does it? Maybe she didn't slap me. But something happened that was like a slap. And that "slap" has had a great deal to do with how I have lived my life, especially with women, and has even occurred in my dreams. That "great mythical slap," on levels far deeper than "true history," determined the way I saw myself as life continued.

Ten years later, I decided that I deserved that "slap." Indeed (as I remembered it then) I had been out of line. I had disrespected mother. And that slap told me that women have a right to self-respect.

It began with the "false" memory of a slap. Yet it changed my life.

Of course, that pubescent teenage kid might not actually have been "out of line." He was just into puberty in those days. No doubt he was feeling angry and violated about a score of incidents. Nevertheless, the "false" memory and the way he processed it became an epoch in his personal growth.

A mythical truth for a lifetime, based on a literal falsehood.

I'll never forget the young woman who returned from three days and nights of fasting with the remarkable story that an eagle had landed next to her while she was sitting alone on a rock. Our skeptical nature said, "O yeah, and rabbits have kittens." But that part of us that understood the transforming nature of memory realized that "truth" or "lie" was not the question. The real question was, what would she do with this memory? How could it serve her behavior?

She called herself "Thunder Eagle" and assumed a thunder-like swagger. She got a lot of mileage out of that memory. Years later, she continued to refer to herself as Thunder Eagle. And it didn't matter if the memory was a truth or a lie—just as long as everybody realized there was a Thunder Eagle sailing above them.

Some memories are grim and full of death. Others are bright and re-deeming. A Catholic kid who grows up in the ghetto with ten brothers and sisters in a fatherless family may harbor a host of dismal memories, and he may consider them to be true whether they be true-to-life or fiction. He may harbor a story, a myth about himself that says, "My father was a violent, faithless man, therefore I am too." This self-characterization will not serve him well. He will act in such a way as to produce more memories that reinforce this negative story about himself.

We cannot force this young man to drop this dangerous quest for negative memories. We can't incarcerate him or beat the violence out of him. The more we force him, the more he will consider himself to be like his father. Resisting, he will become violent. The subjective truth of his memories will grow stronger. He will continue to see himself as a violent man.

We can, however, provide the young man with other memories and brighter scenarios. We can show him another "truth" about himself, a truth upon which he can base a new or amended story about himself.

This we have done for many years, in the form of rites of passage in the wilderness. The young people return with new memories which, because they were forged in the initiatory fire, are strong and self-motivating.

Many years ago, a young woman came to us who called herself a "chronic liar." We wondered what she meant by that. If no one knows whether you are telling the truth or telling a lie, then no one's able to decide whether you are telling a truth or a lie.

Did she mean to say, "I can't be trusted?" Or did she mean to say, "My memory can't be trusted?" No doubt she had lied to survive. She had gone to jail several times for forging bad checks and shady business deals. But the thing she was about to do—fasting for four days and nights alone in the desert wilderness—was not forge-able. She would be at the mercy of her memories. We figured we had a chance to see how well she danced with the subjective truth of her memories, and told her, "What's the difference? Lie if you want to. We'll believe anything you say."

The idea satisfied her enormously. We wouldn't judge her. We wouldn't care whether she told the truth or a lie. She could be exactly who she was. She could live her "lie" as her story.

When she returned from liminal space, she had interacted with the memory fields of the wind, creosote, a few blue belly lizards, a hawk, a hummingbird, a dove, the desert paintbrush, and sixteen thousand ants. She spoke of the hardships of her ordeal, the boredom, the fantasies, the depressions, the moments of insight. Her dusty clothes clung to her like silence, stars, and dreams. Her story didn't sound much more exaggerated or untrue than any other. We believed every word of it.

Even if everything she said was a lie, it was a good lie, an adequate lie, and promised lies with even more meat in them.

Let us build our future on adequate lies.

❖❖❖❖

Last night, the waiter in a restaurant told us that, as a single father, he had been working all day. We both expressed sympathy, and then wondered if he was telling us this because he hoped for a bigger tip. We laughed and decided to treat him as though he were telling us a real story. We left him a sizable tip.

Later, I got to thinking about that waiter. It seemed to me he was no different than me. I put myself out there into the world. Sometimes it's the truth, sometimes it's a piece of the truth, sometimes it's whatever I can say to make the most of—or side step—the situation that confronts me.

I do not consider this tendency to make the most of any situation, or to gain from it financially or otherwise, to be something recent in the human psyche. This tendency—gift?—is at the soul of Odysseus.

Please, no cynicism! We are cousins to the Coyote. Nature is our mother. We do whatever we can to survive. And if we can, we survive well. And if we have to side step, well, we can dance spellbindingly if we have to.

No doubt there are many bloated with too much who live among us, and yet they are greedy to lie for more. Verily, their lies are only as hopeful as the trajectory of the arrow of their lives. If the arrow flies for the good of us all, then the lie is not only permissible but absolutely necessary. If the arrow flies toward their own liver, well, their aim was pretty bad.

I'll never forget the day I decided to do this work. I had just been in Death Valley with my probation officer friend Tim and a pack of juvenile delinquents. The experience had been a real ordeal. Several of the kids refused the challenge of aloneness in the wilderness. Instead, they had congealed into a rat pack roaming through the desert looking for cars to break into. One kid refused to come back. He took off with his backpack for Las Vegas, 90 miles away. Only three kids actually completed the ceremony, which involved staying alone without food in the desert for two days and nights.

I was driving back across the Golden Gate Bridge, finally alone in the van, when it hit me like a bolt of lightning. I would do this kind of work. I would be—I was—a "vision quest guide."

Ha! Inflated with this lofty story about myself, I was fated to discover that I was nothing but a neophyte, a greenhorn of the first degree. I had just endured a week in the wilderness that could definitely be called a failure. It would take years of apprenticeship, years of mistake-making, years of experimentation and blundering, before I would actually be worthy to call myself a vision quest guide.

Looking back at this moment, I realize that I was defining myself according to certain memories I had of myself. These memories would hardly have qualified me to be an expert. Yet they were enough—false and hazy as they might have been—to drive the engine of my later years, to bring me through 31 years of fumbling, to this day, when I am able to make a more modest claim:

I am learning how to be a vision fast guide. Thirty-one years based on what was essentially a lie. Thirty one years from nothing more than a "wish."

The word "myth" comes from the Greek *muthos* or "ethos of the mouth." "Ethos" is defined as "disposition," "character," or "nature." I like the connotation of nature. The "nature" of the mouth is to speak myth, to utter "mythos."

Mythos is not based on physical reality or fact. But it would be wrong to assume that it is therefore false. Mythos bespeaks a power equal to the influence of the physical world—a power that in fact has a great deal to do with how we dance with our mortal lives.

It is our "nature" to make up stories about our existence, our destiny, and to explain a multitude of tragedies and epiphanies in terms that do not honor scientific objectivity. Why should this be? Is it somehow important and necessary for us to be this way? Long have our ancestors pondered this question.

The stories we tell about our existence are genetically connected to our survival as a species. And I wonder if the universe itself was created out of the same urge to have a story in order to survive.

One important myth of the western world goes that God spoke: "Let there be light." And light sprang from the "muthos" of God. At first, it was pure myth, the wish that light could be. From the wish sprang the reality. "And there was light." God wanted light to be and lo! Light *was!*

Why did the idea of creating the universe ever occur to God? He/She must have remembered that there was such a thing as light. It must have been stored in His/Her memory banks. From the memory came the expression, the story, the fiction. From the fiction came the reality—light.

I can imagine God sitting there in the primordial darkness wishing She/He could see. She/He kept wishing and wishing and then it occurred to Her/Him. "Isn't there something called light?"

Wordsworth said, "We half-create what we perceive." We also half-create what we remember. The other half we don't create with. We simply forget. What is forgotten sinks back into the sea of memory, to be remembered another time.

The fact that we can actually create from our memories proves that we are akin to whatever exists in the *mind* or *soul* of the universe that must bring memories into being, and so re-create (re-member).

According to Judeo-Christianity, God created the universe with the Word (ethos of the mouth). According to the Paiute, Coyote created the universe with song (ethos of the mouth). According to the Aborigines of Australia, the Rainbow Serpent created the universe with names (ethos of the mouth). Where did God find the words? Where did Coyote get the song? Where did the Rainbow Serpent find the names? They remembered.

How can this be? How can we remember from before there was anything to remember? How can something come from nothing? How can a word come from invisibility, inscrutability—from no-thing?

Memory exists perennially in all the solitary, discreet, related, grouped, and interconnected species who owe their existence to Mother Earth. Memory is an invisible ocean, surrounding us, entering us, and enriching the very biochemicals of which our cells are composed. Memory is our Mother and our Father. They remembered God by copulating, and we, and all our brothers and sisters, were born—to remember that we are all related.

From the time we are born, We Who Have Gone Before remember.

What we don't know, we fake.

If I'm driving on a gloomy, rain-drenched night and the windshield wipers are smearing back and forth and I can't see very well if there's an elk or a cow in the road, I fake it.

If I'm standing at the edge of a sheer, dry waterfall and I'm not sure my descent is going to be secure, I fake it.

Faking is one of the two most important functions of memory. Knowing absolutely for certain is the second. The border between the two is quite indistinct.

If I fake something successfully—that is, if I fake it until I realize that I knew how to all along, then something in me feels grateful—like when I go to some place where I was afraid to go and find that being there feels not only familiar but downright homey. Like when a person in pain is standing before me and I don't know what to say to her—and if, in my dismay, the way gradually becomes clear, I ascribe this power to god, or spirit, or some unseen agency working its magic within me. At such times, I am grateful to know that another name for God is Faking It.

❖❖❖❖

The time has come to write my will. I leave behind everything to my wife, my children, my grandchildren—any tangible possession, any concrete symbol of karma, everything insubstantial as only memories can be. Accumulations. Body baggage—trash to be burned. Do with my karma as you will. Dear Lord, what a load of shit I leave behind!

To my children and my grandchildren, I bequeath my genes, dominant and recessive, the light and shadow of the double helix of memory. I give you We Who Have Gone Before, the path I traveled in life, my Yellow Brick Road. You will walk your own road, and you will certainly learn from your pilgrimages. Also, I bequeath to you my imagination, the arts of remembering dawn, and the arts of remembering dusk.

I will my memory-heart, and my memory-heartlessness, to my woman. Genital memories too. They were much attached to her. I guess I'd be willing to give her everything, because that's just what I did in this life. I gave her my soul. But by now I'm having a hard time figuring out whose soul is whose. I bequeath to her *our* soul. Our memories. Our life together.

To all my loving friends, to those who live in recollection as angels, demons, lovers, compadres, competitors, colleagues, and teachers, I leave all those loving words and deeds left untold, all those embraces ignored or turned aside, all those hopes and dreams we didn't share together, everything I forgot to say.

The Old English word "mourn" is related to the Latin *memor* or "mindful." Be mindful of me, dearest ones. Mourn for my life, and be mindful of my death.

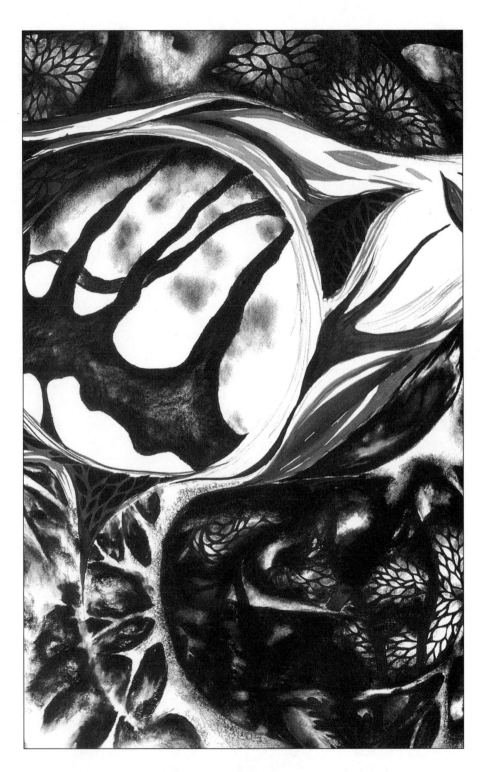

Selene Foster: Charcoal on paper, '98

THE BIG ONE

Sometimes, when I'm alone in the wilderness, I get hungry for sex. Most people do. Animal, vegetable, and mineral surround, permeate, and quicken our deepest memories with perfectly natural urges. Our species would not otherwise have survived. We always tell people not to be ashamed of the desire to pleasure themselves while they are alone and fasting in liminal space. Everything that happens there is sacred. Everything. Sacred masturbation. Sacred fantasy. Sacred shit.

Solitary Proustian excursions into memory to retrieve sensations (imagined or desired), events (actual or fantastic), people (real or fictitious), to give ourselves pleasure, are like fishing for the BIG ONE. I'm not just talking sex. We do this all the time, to make ourselves feel good in all kinds of ways.

It's like the art of angling. Maybe I'll catch something that will feed me and my loved ones.

When you go fishing you have to bait your hook. Then you throw it in the stream and wait for a strike. Wham! A huge shadow in the pool takes the bait. With trembling hands you reel it in. There it is. You can see it. A BIG ONE. With care and luck you finally bring the prize into capture. A rainbow flops and shimmers on the bank.

Memory is where the BIG ONE lives. And what you catch depends on the way you bait your hook, and the way you play your line out into the current. No matter what bait you put on the hook, it is always a memory-worm. You fish for the BIG ONE with a memory worm.

Sometimes you get a strike when you least expect it. You're not even aware that you've been fishing. You're walking along, hardly mindful of the images flooding your head, and whack!—all of a sudden you're whistling "Amazing Grace," or some such thing, and light trembles everywhere like leaves quaking on an aspen, and you're being masturbated in four dimensions by memory.

Sometimes you fish for a long time, trying to retrieve you know not what, scanning the endless shores of memory like a castaway sailor far from shore. And all around you is blackness, bleakness, inscrutability, and you are sure no BIG ONE dwells in these waters.

Sometimes you catch a BIG ONE and you don't even know it, distracted by events of the moment, by other memories of a negative kind, by indifference.

Sometimes the BIG ONE slaps you in the face and you still don't see it.

And sometimes it isn't the BIG ONE that takes the bait. It's a minnow, or a polliwog, or a junk fish, only remotely related to the BIG ONE. And sometimes you're thankful because at least you caught something—or sometimes you are so disappointed you throw it back.

Obviously, we can't always stash the BIG ONE in our creel. But we keep on trying. It's the idea of going fishing that lures us. We remember the last time we caught a BIG ONE and we can't resist. Memory craves memory.

This craving must have resulted in creation. And lo!, the BIG ONE lay flopping in the abyss of night, shining like a billion galaxies.

I think as we get older and closer to death we go fishing for the BIG ONE more often. I may be wrong about this. The rule may not apply to people with Alzheimer's. But now that I am headed toward 70, I have noticed a tendency within myself to savor the past more than I did when I was a young sprout. It might just be that old age brings more patience to stand there on the bank of the river fishing for BIG ONES.

Old age can also bring obsession, fixation on particular events in the past. My father, who is nearing 90, keeps catching the same fish over and over again. It's a mining tunnel he blasted into the side of Shadow Mountain when he was 18. He wants to go back there, to late adolescence, when life held so much potential, before he met my mother and WW II arrived and they had four kids in quick succession. Every time I talk with him he says he wants to go back to Shadow Mountain, to take a look at the "east end tunnel."

The east end tunnel, where the sun rises in the morning? Maybe that's why I keep fishing for those Big Ones. Like my father, I am on the arduous journey to death. Along the way I have to catch a BIG ONE to carry me across the threshold, a prize so big it will pull me in—and I will merge with the depths of the great river of memory and travel as far and wide as I can.

I know what I'm fishing for. But so far the BIGGEST ONE has eluded me.

Sometimes I think the river I'm fishing these days is called Eros. The bait I'm using is my relationship with M and all the other women I've known. I'm reasonably convinced that the BIGGEST ONE is even now sniffing my bait. I like to think of her as feminine, beautiful, deadly, and wise beyond comprehending. She will lift her skirt and I'll see what's underneath. It will be impossible to resist her. Before I know it I'll be flopping in her creel. I'd rather be a rainbow than a junk fish.

WE WHO HAVE GONE BEFORE

Imagine yourself as a Polynesian navigator sailing an outrigger from Hawaii to Tahiti or Samoa, traversing thousands of miles of Pacific Ocean without compass or sextant, steering with a certain half-remembered knowledge stored in your memory. Could you do it? Maybe not, despite the fact that this ability still lies buried in our collective psyche. I like the metaphor anyway.

Those great Pacific navigators, those hardy ancestors who steered by the stars, tides, wind, currents, sun, rain, clouds, birds, dolphins, fish—ah, they were a select bunch! If I had another life to lead, I would go back in time and live as one of those. Their journeyings comprise one of the great archetypal passages in the human mind—from *here* to *there*. The great rites of passage.

Every day we find ourselves adrift on the great sea of memory. For days, weeks at a time, the seas are calm, the days sunny, the trade winds fair, the sails full, and all we have to do is steer automatically—remembering "how we sailed before."

But suddenly the surface of the sea will change. Monsters rise from the deep: whirlpools, rapids, doldrums, black holes, riptides, undertows, lightning and thunder, typhoon winds, flash flooding rain. The stars will be blotted out and all will seem lost. We will hang on to our puny craft for dear life and pray for mercy. Nature will respond, but not always with mercy.

For how many eons have we lashed ourselves to the tiller and steered into the jaws of death? But never did we sail blindly. Automatic recollections tensed our muscles and nerves. We became sensitive to the slightest tolerances of the wheel. Can we be forgiven for remembering, in the fury of the moment, that we owed our survival to We Who Have Gone Before?

I want to go back in time to understand how deeply those old Polynesian mystics plumbed the wisdom of their hallowed ancestors. I want to swim in their intuition and steer by their symbols. I want to feel the ancient tugging of the great passage. I want to remember what they remembered, experience what they experienced, go where they dared.

And when the dawn rises on the silhouette of a distant island, I want to cry from relief and weigh anchor in the nearest cove. I want to arrive at home.

Where do tears come from? Why do our children, even our tiny babies, shed tears? No doubt there are many biological/psychological theories. But no one knows for sure.

When we were living in Greece, on the island of Ithaka, we witnessed the ceremonial sacrifice of a goat in celebration of a baptism. Because we had the only car in town, the people of our village asked us to bring the sacrificial goat down from its home on Mt. Neion. The man who rode with us was careful to keep the goat facing away from the direct sunlight. "She must not look into the sun," he said, "or she will cry."

All attempts to keep her from crying were doomed when the sacrificial knife appeared. She saw it coming—and she wept.

I will never forget the deft slit-stroke that severed her jugular vein. At that moment I knew beyond the shadow of a doubt that during the feast that followed, we would have to taste the meat—even M, who was vegetarian. We would have to partake of communion, in the eating of the slain goddess who shed her blood and her tears that the people of her town might live another year.

Almost without thinking, we were enacting a ritual as ancient as We Who Have Gone Before—the celebration of complicity in the sacrifice of an "innocent one." We were formally acknowledging our own mortality. Someday the knife would appear at our throats.

And the tears? We Who Have Wept Before.

Many years ago, in the midst of personal crisis (loss of employment and separation from children), while sleeping alone in the desert, I had a dream, and awoke flooded with light. It seems I had been standing on a hillside looking into the rising sun, and a group of people had been there with me. There was nothing unusual about any of us. Just ordinary people waiting for the sun to rise. Even so, there was some kind of unspoken joy between us, so deep and pervasive as to awake me in a fit of rapturous tears.

Thirty years later, having accompanied thousands of people into the wilderness to wait for the sun to rise on the last morning of a sacred fast, I know who these dream people were. They were We Who Have Gone Before.

Time, Fossils, Lithic Scatter

The river of time flows down from the Mountains of Now and empties into the Sea of Memory. What is becomes was, and what was always becomes memory. Time, as a subjective flow of consciousness, erodes the banks of the objective world. Infinitely persistent, the river flows, carrying pieces of now all the way to the great sea of forever.

Time is the midwife of memory. Time nurtures, feeds, and hallows memory. The future will emerge from memory's open mouth. Memory will eat the future becoming present and will swallow it down into the intestines of the past. There it will melt into the Sea of Memory—where, in storm and calm, the Word will come forth.

You say you want to be a princess or a prince, a magician or a clown; you want to travel, see the world, get a job, be somebody, have the ultimate orgasm? Then what you're really talking about is memory. You're saying that the future craves to be remembered, no matter how we go about remembering it. We want to live so badly, we want to savor, to redeem ourselves from the past!

Does time ever stop helping space give birth to memories? Never. Memory must always permeate space. . . . so that space will forever remember time.

You may think your life is too long. But when you come to the end you may think it too short. You may wonder how you lived without being truly able to savor the memories. Now at the end you hardly have time to go back. To do that would take another lifetime. And you have only this one.

Given the way you remember your life, would you say it was worth it? Would you have gained a pretty good idea of why you happened to wind up here? Could you identify the memories in the stories that tell the saga of you?

Could it be that one of the main reasons we are on this earth is to remember who we are?

The song that sings in our blood, the song of our sacred ancestors, transcends the boundaries of a lifetime. Memories make a mockery of such ephemeral borders as future, present, and past. We Who Have Gone Before always remember who we are, any time, anywhere.

My father wrote his retirement thesis on the subject of Space/Time. An amateur mathematician, he was intrigued for 50 years by challenges future astronauts would face when they piloted space vehicles capable of the speed of light. When I first read his treatise, "Voyage at C," I was astounded. This man had a profound grasp of the special theory of relativity. He had effectively reduced Lorentz transformations, the appearance of fast moving meter sticks, the addition and subtraction of velocities approaching c, and gravitation, to simple problems in trigonometry. He assumed that every object in the universe is aging at the absolute speed of light, and that there is no motion in space except that produced by angular tilting of time axes. His computations were mathematically correct to 16 decimal places on the computer of a professor of physics at the University of Victoria.

When he submitted his thesis to the *American Journal of Physics*, with state of the art diagrams, they requested permission to transfer his copyright to them. He agreed. Months later, he received another letter: the article wasn't publishable; it was too long; they would keep a copy on file at Washington University in St. Louis.

I always wondered why this man, who made parts for spacecraft in his tool and die shop, should have been so interested in the theory of relativity. Now I understand. While the years passed and he drilled perfect holes in intricate form blocks, he was listening to We Who Have Gone Before. They whispered to him that we were all moving at the speed of light, and that there was no motion in space save for the angular tilting of time axes.

After a lifetime in the Inyo-Mojave, I've come to think of fossils as anything dead for over a year. The dry winds and searing heat mummify within a month. I looked for a long time at an old time photo of a man who had died in the summer heat of Death Valley. He had a hideous grin on his face.

I hold the image of his face in my mind. I think he was trying to say, "We are all fossils."

The measuring stick of memory reduces time to a process whereby what happens today becomes a past organically connected to tomorrow. Nowhere is this fact more clear than in the desert.

A vision faster returned from the Eureka Valley with the report that she had come across a dead rattlesnake. The head had been eaten away by ravens. The vertebrae and skull were blackened by sun, rain, and fungus. But the rest of the body was intact, down to ten perfect rattles.

To my mind, that rattlesnake was a fossil. And in it one could read thousands, even millions of years, of geologic time.

"Rattlesnake-ness." When did it all begin? We could trace the pit vipers way back to the appearance of reptiles. But that would not end our search. Rattlesnake-ness has been an urge of Mother Nature from the time she was conceived—or, should I say, remembered?

Humans haven't been around very long, considering the age of Mother Earth—and we're just one of those billions of species she remembered to put here. On the vast stage of evolutionary time we are no more special than the squirrel, or the sparrow, or the skunk beetle, or any new species even now in the process of being remembered.

Mother Earth seems to have remembered us fairly recently in the game. The fact that we are new hardly changes our importance. She can remember, and she can forget.

I try to imagine the future of the human race. We've come quite a way along our species time line. But we could disappear in an instant. In fact, we are very close to doing just that. What difference would that make to Great Mother Nature? Billions of species have appeared. Billions have winked out. The fossil record teaches us all that we need to know. We are not the GREAT EXPERIMENT. We are simply another combination in her genetic memory, evolving like everything else in the universe.

Time means nothing to the Great Mother. What do fossils really teach us? The oldest records point to a worm-like creature living three and a half billion years ago, at the threshold of geologic time—the first ancestor of the human species, and not a short-lived one. That tight little coil of life survived for hundreds of millions of years. In comparison, the survival span of homo sapiens is but a snap of the fingers. Which species was/is more adapted?

Will Mother forget to let us live? And will it be such a terrible thing if she does?

Why then am I so afraid to die? Why, with every motion, do I grasp like a rock climber for tiny handholds on the cliffs of breath? Could it be that Mother actually remembered to give all life this same fear of losing hold? Why would she do such a thing? If she plays fast and loose with the destinies of all the species, why would she instill in us such a fear of non-becoming?

Took a walk today in the Last Chance Mountains. Limestone and igneous rock everywhere. Volcanoes and ancient sea beds. Everything breaking down into calcium, carbon, silica, and gasses which, combined with other gasses, compose the vital components of the air we breathe.

Now I sit behind the tailgate of the old Ford and watch the darkness swallow the white dolomite of Last Chance Peak. A nearby BLM marker formally reminds me. I am at the boundary of "WILDERNESS." I'm a long way from nowhere. If I tried to walk out of here I'd probably have to surrender my body to the death change.

How about "WILDERNESS" in a different sense—wilderness as "change?" The way everything is remembering to be what it is always becoming—other elements, substances, entities. Mountains crumbling into air.

I can see the value of blissing out on who I am. But too many people are coming to us, wanting to be someone else. What do we tell them? To resist change? Even the rocks seem to be remembering how much they want to become a gas. What chance does a frail being like me stand against the forces of change?

For twenty years I've picked up shards of obsidian, chert, and chalcedony left on the ground hundreds of years ago by Native American stone tool makers. I look for a certain shape—flat, thin, and round enough to pressure flake into bird points. I have made thousands of points from the leavings of the old Indian arrowhead artists.

Years ago, I used the sharp tips of deer or elk horn to shape the point. But the horn tips kept getting duller and I had to continually work at resharpening them with water and sandstone. I almost heeded the advice of an old Miwok arrow maker who advised me to use copper wire. I thought about that for a long time, about what wire meant, archeology-wise, and decided instead to use a ten penny nail.

I'm attracted to the old Stone Age ways. I can weave an acceptable willow basket, twist lengths of milkweed fiber or sinew into a strong rope, start a fire in cottonwood tinder with a bow drill, stalk a deer, catch a fish with a hook made of bird bone, kill, skin and eat a rattlesnake, eat a grub, fletch and fashion a compound arrow, shape a birch or willow bow with obsidian flakes, identify and reap edible roots, plants, and berries, bake pemmican, cook pine nut and choke cherry mush . . . . I could survive on the land if my lungs were operable.

I'm so happy to be remembering.

Stone tool making goes back a long way. My mind boggles at the centuries. A thousand? A hundred thousand? No doubt the first artisans were motivated by extreme hunger. They realized the stones they were using to club their prey to death could be sharpened. It probably took thousands of years of dreaming, thinking about "killing sharpness." Then one day a man (it could have been a woman) did it, hardly thinking about what he/she was doing. He/she simply remembered what all the others gone before had been trying to remember.

Our revolutionary ancestor picked up a stone to shape into a hammer. The first time, the stone being shaped probably broke—or the hammer stone broke. But by then the hunter could sense how he/she might go about being successful. Once the trick was done, the cat was out of the bag. The news must have spread faster throughout the earth than gold rush fever.

Stone tools seem to have lasted almost forever. Only recently in the history of We Who Have Gone Before did copper, tin, iron, gunpowder, and finally nuclear and biochemical poisons, prevail as the weapons of choice.

No doubt this lasting value is why the surface of the desert is littered with all those artificially shaped pieces of stone. For such a long time that was all there was. Stone. Mineral. Rudimentary petrology.

If war has to be, I would much rather be shot with an obsidian arrow point than a poison capsule. And if war must forever be, I would much rather be killed by a sober-minded elder than a hot young blood stoned out of his gourd on patriotism and self-righteousness.

After twenty-five years of chipping, flaking, grinding, shaping, I can say without equivocation that I would never have taken up such a profession if it had not been for a memory somehow graven in my genes by my white Indian ancestors. The old Paiute Indian doctor seemed to take this white-man obsessively-chipping-points in stride. He didn't consider me to be an Indian wannabe. He was only interested in the pieces that took shape from the horn and leather. Once he saw that they were passable as hunting implements, he didn't get pissed at me for stealing his culture. One memorable day he told me he thought that this white man chipping was probably okay, and he wanted to know where I had picked up those chunks of obsidian. "Glass Mountain," I said.

"Yeah. That's a good place. Have you been down to Fish Springs?"

"No."

"Check it out," he said. At that moment, I realized he respected me for remembering my white ancestors. And he was right. There was some real good stuff around Fish Springs.

The elders have been flaked to a point by the horn of life. Did they always do the right thing? Of course not. The elders are human. But they are something more than human. They are beings who have suffered. They know a hell of a lot more than those young whippersnappers who still have to be tested in the lists of fire. Sure, maybe the old guys froze into an attitude of "conservative" or "liberal." Maybe they even seem nothing more than "old farts" who storm and rage in teapots. But they have been whacked hard by the hammer, and they have lived and survived somehow, even if they had to use the bottle to get through. Give them some space. Let them have their say. It could very well be that they know more than we think they do.

When did we begin to discount wisdom just because it came from the mouth of an old cripple, or an old man who lost his wife, or an old widow who raised a dozen children, or an old woman who made pots for 40 years, or an old man who worked on car engines, or mucked in a mine all his life? Elders are obsidian tools that have endured incessant hammer strokes, any one of which could have shattered them into pieces. They are survivors: strapped to a hardwood point by circumstance, attached to the feathers of a bird, and shot into the blue distances of life and time. If we discount what they remember, we are fools.

The young have always picked up the current technology as easily as worms pick up soil. Back in the Stone Age, it was all that how-to-survive-in-the-wilderness technology: hunting, gathering, preserving, cooking, sheltering, childbearing, curing and healing, migrating, etc. By the time they were 16, they knew enough to at least rudimentarily operate a multitude of technological systems, from arrow-making to curing the common cold.

Even today, in Mr. Todd's fourth grade class, I see the same potential. Instantaneously, they understand the principles of fire-making, fiber-twisting, and the shaping of stone. There has been no lapse in their genes. Even the crudest attempts by an abused 10-year-old are certain testimony to this ancient, ancestral memory. The kids don't do this because they are supposed to do it. They do it because they are enjoying the remembrance of doing it.

So I keep trying to find the connection between the past and the present. It is, after all, nothing but remembering. If our children remember how to flake points, they also remember how to use the current technology in order to survive. Unfortunately, they are also remembering how to self-destruct—how to fashion tools into weapons of species destruction, genocide, terrorism, and self-obliteration.

The only really significant difference between the Stone Age technologies and their computer age equivalents is the modern lack of rites of entry into maturity, competence, and responsibility. No longer does the technology require the mastery of an initiated adult. There are too few to say, "This is the way to make a point, and this is not the way to make a point. This is the way to hunt, and that is not the way to hunt. This is the way to be of use to us. This is not the way to be of use to us. This is the way of mastering, and this is not the way. This is the way of becoming a man or a woman, and this is not the way of becoming a man or a woman."

Technology, a sophisticated form of the binary system, is simply technology, neither good nor evil. In the hands of uninitiated men or women, it will kill us.

MONEY

When it comes to us freely? Or when it comes to us because we worked hard for it?

When we have just enough? Or when we are haunted by those who have less?

When what we have doesn't seem nearly enough to cover our old age and death? Or when we see an opportunity to bestow grace and blessing in dollars and cents to those special people who will live beyond us?

Money is karma. Money is love. Money is indifference. Money is play. Money is gratitude. Money is hope. Money is greedily and deceptively acquired. Money is favor. Money is everything and nothing. Money is the staff of life. Money has a conscience. Money is the devil. Money is God. Money is everything but God or the devil. Lack of money causes death.

Money is survival, at any level of luxury, from a makeshift shelter to a yacht-like mansion. Money defines us, stereotypes us, teaches us, fills us, empties us, deludes us. Money comes alike to those who dream it and those who do not dream it.

Money does not care much for the stuff beneath our feet, yet it is composed of the stuff beneath our feet. Money is what we have converted this earth into, only to discover that there is absolutely no difference between earth and us. Money dies. Money lives. Nature dies. Nature lives. Like nature itself, money is married to people. But money nature doesn't want to be married to people. Money separates, divorces, marries again. Money is a fickle satyr. Money is a saint. Money gives life. Money murders. Money slips around like coyote.

Money is memory, a way of acquiring memories, of acquitting memories, a way of feeling and a way of not feeling. Money is the medium of exchange between our sacred ancestors: If I give you this, you give me that. Money is body, psyche, mind, and spirit. Money is not body, psyche, mind, and spirit. Money is money.

And how do we console ourselves at the moment of death? With money?

Only the memories money has given us will accompany us through the gates of death. Money shapes the next life.

And the first monster we encounter in the death passage will be money.

There was a wealthy man in Austria who decided he would walk along a busy street in Reid and give money away. He was certain he would be happier afterward. For hours he stopped people to give money to them. Some were surprised and grateful. Some were suspicious and outraged. Others were puzzled and undecided. Over half of those to whom he offered money would not accept it.

In time he discovered he was being followed by a crowd of children. They had heard about the man giving money away and wanted their share. They became so obnoxious that, in exasperation, he told them: "Only those who don't ask will get money."

After that, the children dogged his footsteps in complete silence.

We all want money. We would like it to come to us freely. But when it is in our grasp, many of us do not want it. Already the children learn how to get it. Act like you don't want it and then, when the give-away man isn't looking, pick his pocket. Or hope beyond hope that he will look back and see the one who is most worthy—me of course—and tenderly beknight my outstretched hands.

Do we really want money? Without it we cannot live. But surely, money is nothing but turds and shells and bits of mineral and whale fat and fresh meat and vegetables, and animals like pigs, cows, dogs, monkeys, deer, and property like slaves, criminals, women, men, children, land, houses, boats, tools, seeds, crops. Money is everything we want and don't want, everything we live with and don't live with.

Do we have any choice?

If we must live with money, then we must decide how to dance with the memory of money, graven so deeply in our genes and reinforced by the morphogenetic fields of human nature. Yes, but how do we dance, how do we give ourselves to the moneyless treasures of life on this island earth and clap our hands with the joyful passing of days—and yet make money, living in a world full of gigantic sharks who gobble up money and pieces of our flesh?

How? Who am I to say? I know nothing about dancing with money, except what I can remember from my distant past as an apelike creature swinging from the trees of an African jungle. When I remember with my ancestor, I know that if I give a banana I may (if I do it right) be the recipient of a banana. I look for bananas; I find bananas; I give my bananas to others; and I get bananas back. Some of the bananas that come to me I eat. But when I am full of banana, I wonder if I will need any more. So I give some of my bananas to other banana hunters, hoping to get back more bananas.

There's this thing about bananas. I don't know exactly where it came from. But it has to do with trusting that there will be some kind of benefit—to me—from the giveaway of my bananas, and that there are real and imaginary bananas.

Is this trust spiritual? Do we actually believe that if we do good, God will reward us? Don't ask me. I've never had quite enough. Yet not quite enough was enough. Maybe we should ask our banana-loving sacred ancestors.

Land is money. When this definition was made by the human consciousness, I myself was hardly around. Maybe 20,000 years ago, who knows? Despite their belief that the earth is Grandmother Earth, even American Indians, Australian Aborigines, South African Zulus, European Celts, had to admit that their particular living, hunting, and gathering grounds had been bequeathed, for profound reasons, to them and their offspring.

Property is livelihood, survival, perpetuity, the breeding ground and teacher of ways to make itself fruitful and to multiply. Property begets money. Property brings the midwives who assist at the birth. Property undergirds the growth of the young. Property provides for the passage of the young into adulthood. Property, and the need to attain it, propels the rocket into the outer space of Maturity. Property is death. Property is home.

Death, Prayer, and DNA

It must be that we remember how to die. I don't buy the theory that modern folks have lost this faculty. We're a couple million years old and we've been dying all that time. My grandfather got it from his grandfather and his grandfather got it from his grandfather, and so on, all the way back. But we just can't access such a memory any time we want to. It's the biggest of those BIG ONES.

Ordinarily, death memory becomes active in our twilight years, or when, regardless of age, we confront the deadly circumstances of a life threatening dis-ease. Certain feelings seem to bring on death memory—alienation, loneliness, and uselessness, psychic and physical pain, exhaustion, fear, despair, guilt—such as these accompany the tugging of mortality.

You can tell if you're remembering. You begin to get curious about what's on the other side. At the same time you're getting sick and weary of this old life—or you're realizing you can't hold on forever, that death is, after all, absolutely necessary. Something irresistible begins to tug at you. You begin to let go. I watched my father and mother consciously begin to relent. I assume I will do it too.

The river of life and time empties into the great sea of memory. Where do we go from here? We go where we remember to go.

My lungs are giving out. A case of pneumonia or bronchitis would kill me. Every day, death memories brush in close and stick to me like milkweed seeds. I may have to say goodbye at any second. My heart pounds in my chest, skips a beat. A scream trembles at the lip of a chasm. I look back and wonder, is this the last look?

But then I come back to my feet. I was on the verge of doing something and I have to do it. The death memory spits out the hook, falls back into the river. No regrets. Something has to be done. Tomorrow the BIG ONE will strike again, and for a moment I will wrestle with the Dark Angel.

Practice, practice. And then one bright day it's not practice anymore.

The loss of a loved one can bring on the most poignant death memories. The odor of mortality hangs heavy in the air. It is a medical truism that among long-married couples, the death of one spouse often impels the death of the other. We miss the departed one. We want to go with her/him. Life no longer seems meaningful without our beloved.

Death memories serve another function. They enhance life for the living. They spin the wheel of the seasons. They provide entrance to a greater cycle. The endless summer of the orgasmic body has passed. Fall came with an inward dying, a shedding of leaves, a feeling of loss. The Garden was gone. Winter was coming. Look how the color of the leaves change from green to gold to black! All summers fall doth end.

The great wheel turns on. Summer prepares to die in the fall. But even as summer prepares to die, we remember that winter will not forever hold us in its icy grip. We will keep ourselves alive in the warm chambers of the seed, in the inner sanctum of the earthworm. As we survive, we will provide for the needs of the people, especially the children and the grandchildren.

And still the great wheel turns. We know it will turn because we remember spring. The grave shall open wide and the spirit shall come forth. The dark passage will unfold like a wild flower.

Beyond the mountains of night, a golden land of mystery lies. The briefest recollection of it stirs the soul. We will rise again like little children from a bed of sleep and walk into the wonder world of summer.

Death reminds us that it is only a spoke in the Great Wheel.

Death is a worthy opponent, the ultimate ally. We engage death with our long term memory—the one that looks back at years of living and growing and making mistakes. When we review our life through our ancestors' eyes we have to face the fact that, in the end, our little life-home doesn't mean shit. Death comes in and takes everything away that isn't invisible. Status attained, goods acquired—the me-ego stuff—all these things death ignores.

And so we are no greater or smaller than all the other creatures who die. Like them, we have to struggle with death—a struggle doomed to failure.

Our only weapons will be our mortal bodies. We will fight death with our wrinkles.

Yes, we can fight, and we must, in order to complete our story, but in the end we have to remember. We will come to the place of skulls, where rot the bones of all the dancers on the great ball court. All.

The Place of Skulls is so vast I couldn't begin to describe it.

The Grim Reaper is too powerful for me. If I venture into the lightning storm happening around the house at this very moment, simply to turn off the water in the garden, I run an incalculable risk of being riveted on the spot. The very idea of being that close to death terrifies and excites me. My life takes on an elemental meaning with certain spiritual over-tones. My senses open to the wind, and my body quivers with the hope of having more.

So I go out into the storm, where I have to go, where I must go. And memory walks with me, reminding me that death can come without warning.

Are we not as rich as a pocket mouse and poor as a spider mite?

William Blake rightly declared, "The road of excess leads to the palace of wisdom." What he didn't say was that the road of excess also leads to the mansion of death.

So what would you have, now that you stand at the edge of the great abyss? A surfeit of too much? Or a feeling of not enough?

One reason why many older people tend to live more simply—certainly they used to—is that they are trying to get accustomed to living with just enough. Not too much. Not too little. Just enough.

Long-term memory does that to you. You can see what it all comes to in the end.

But when you're young, you don't remember much in the long term. Blake's advice is wonderful for young folks leaving home to find out who they are, seeking all kinds of exciting rites of passage into adulthood. *Carpe diem.* Some never even want to reach adulthood. They would rather be addicted to the short term. I'm reminded of a young basketball player I coached who said, "I'm going to party forever!" Three years later he had a wife and two children.

Like I say, maybe for the young. But not for those who, in old age, are packing the karma of years of behavior. Better for them to temper their excess with wisdom. "The best wine is the oldest, the best water the newest." (Blake)

There's nothing wrong with going on a binge every once in a while, no matter how old we are. Death doesn't mind sitting up in the stands and applauding how well we dance. And is it not true that we dance better when death plays the tune?—when we know that life will never come around exactly this way again?

It seems to me that "too much" and "not enough" are related. They are both sides of the same coin. Death memory recognizes that either position is untenable. Death takes "too much" and renders it "not enough." Death takes "not enough" and renders it "too much."

What is life that it should be so heedless of death? And what is death that it should be so heedless of life? Opposite sides of the same coin. But where was the coin minted?

In the Underworld? Dark is only one half of light.

In Heaven? Light is only one half of dark.

The coin is tarnished with age, beyond recognition.

Surely, Heaven and Hell are the proverbial married couple. They need each other. They must have each other. They cannot get along without each other. They cannot get along with each other. When they are together they fight and make love and blame each other for their problems. They have falling-outs. And then they make up.

Life is not sacred and profane. Life is sacredprofane. When we look back on the history of our people, we see this. In the quietude of our hearts we remember life calling us, like a song on the radio you can't turn off, like a bird, singing from a limb, who never flies away, like a mosquito who keeps coming back for more. Sacredprofane. It rolls off the tongue like honeyed garbage. This is our lot in life. To live in the darkness and the light, to want too much and never have enough, to fuck God and worship the Devil.

In the movies, people die like flies. The villain almost always gets it in the end—occasionally the hero. Everybody else lives on, apparently happily, now that the big trouble is over. We switch off, go to bed—and in the middle of the night we awaken with nightmares.

Dream death of the screen is something quite different than real death. Not that there are no exceptions. Most of the time we accept screen death as make-believe, especially when the villain goes down for the count. Why shouldn't the bad guys get it in the end? What about the good guys? Well, they get it in the end too, but they die happily—right?

Like me, like the way I'll die. A warm mist will take me—or I'll be holding hands with my loved ones—or it'll be sudden, like a sharp pain, and then I'll be gone without misery—or I'll die peacefully in my sleep. Angels will come for me. Actually, I wonder how I will actually die.

Death is very personal—nothing like the death in someone else's story. Death is for *me*. Sure, for everybody else too, but in the end, they are of less importance to me than I am to me. Even my beloved life partner must be left behind, my children, my grandchildren, my life-time dreams!

Perhaps one of the truest questions posed by film is: am I a villain or a hero? If I am a villain, I deserve it real bad. If I am a hero, it would be a terrible tragedy if I were to die. For God's sake, let me be a hero!

But I'm a villain too. And someday soon I will just be one of those Who Have Gone Before.

I often marvel why humans pray, given Mother Nature's apparent insensitivity to human concerns. She does what she does, regardless of how we might feel about it. For example, when I plant seeds in the garden, I pray

Selene Foster: Mixed media on paper, '99

that they will break from the soil, grow strong, and provide sustenance for my family. Every day I "pray with my feet," carefully tending the garden to make certain those first sprouts appear. Finally, I'm rewarded for my efforts. The seedlings burst into light. I exult: "My prayers have been answered! Thank you Grandmother!"

The next day, the sprouts are gone. The quail have eaten every last one.

I can kick and scream and lose my faith, but I know that Nature has her way. She'd just as soon feed the birds as feed my family.

That's not the only example of how Mother Nature doesn't answer prayer. Several years ago, Ted, a vision quest midwife and a friend of ours, went hiking alone above the Hilton Lakes in late spring. He slipped on a boulder and broke his leg, his pelvis, and several ribs. That same night a storm swept in. The mercury dropped below zero. A week later, when the freeze relented, they found his body frozen into a fetal position.

I still feel Ted's despair. He prayed so hard. He prayed until his lips froze and his heart ceased to beat. If God or the spirits of that place heard his prayers, they did nothing. They let him die.

It hurts to go on. Something in me doesn't want to accept the facts. Something in me persists in believing the efficacy of prayer. I wonder why I hold such an irrational belief. Is it simply a cultural attitude bred into me at a young age? Or is there some reason, however intangible, for prayer to exist?

In the dark of night, when I awake from sleep and become aware that I've been slowly strangling from lack of air, I pray for life. I tell myself that if I pray, somehow everything will be all right.

Can it be that prayer is a memory built into every living organism by Mother Nature? Could it be that we all remember to pray for life, for another breath, even at the very moment we are being forced to accept the inevitable? If so, prayer may have more to do with where we go after we die than saving us for this mortal life.

Every time I ask, I get a different answer. I think our definition of prayer depends on what is happening at the time. If we are happy, prayer is a means of expressing gratitude. If we are unhappy, prayer is a means of lamenting. If we are desperate, prayer is a means of calming. If we feel empty, prayer is a means of ingesting. If we feel full, prayer is a means of emptying.

I once asked Grandpa, our Paiute Indian doctor and teacher, how to pray. He said, "Prayer is bullshittin'. You don't need no fancy words. You just bullshit with the spirits." By "spirits" he meant all living things. To him, spirit didn't exist apart from palpable entities. And every spirit was an expression of Grandmother Earth and Great Grandfather.

I like what Grandpa said, very much. I can see how, by his definition, I am praying all the time. It is easy to bullshit with a lizard, or a thunderstorm. And it is just as easy to to kick back and bullshit as it is to raise my fist and defy.

You say you need more of the "sacred" so you can pray humble and beautiful prayers to the assembled multitudes? I'm not sure what you mean by "sacred." Too often, when I knelt in the cathedral of wilderness like a supplicant in a prayer meeting, I felt cramped and awkward. Why should the Great Spirit expect me to feel physically uncomfortable in His/Her presence? Surely, He/She would much rather that I took my ease and conversed irrationally about what was going on. Do I have the right to get angry or desperate? No doubt. Does the Great Mystery have the right to ignore me and talk about something else? No doubt. The Great Mystery always finds a way to answer prayers.

Prayer can be therapy. You're talking to the Great Therapist in the Sky. You tell him/her all your troubles. He/she simply listens—every now and then saying, "Uh, huh," or "How does that make you feel?"

Can we help it that the Great Therapist was trained in "nondirective listening?" You'd think the Expert will solve your problems for you. Fat chance. You'll probably be able to solve your problems for yourself, in one way or another. If you're really desperate, the best you can hope for is a miracle.

Whatever we do with our faith, we must not disparage miracles. They are organically connected to us. They happen every day, every hour, every second. They happen when we work for them so hard we finally reach the borders of despair.

If you remember this, the Great Therapist in the Sky cannot help but remember too. There will be a moment of deep insight between you. It will be beautiful and tragic. You will laugh and cry together. Then your Therapist will say, "I think you're strong enough to go on."

I keep going back to all those nights alone and hungry, looking up at the stars. Memories of my loved ones always come to mind. In my imagination I live with them for a while, even as my eyes drink the Milky Way.

I don't know if my loved ones are aware at those moments that I am praying for them. No matter. I love them anyway.

We create the way we die, even if we are dying from an inherited disease. We shape our destiny with shadow prayers.

Shadow prayers are the ways we pray for death, by our actions, our thoughts, even our hidden longings. If we are physical, we are also psychological, mental, and spiritual. We make mythologies of our dying. These mythologies can be intensely personal, never shared with anyone else but We Who Have Gone Before.

The New Age prayer guru says these mythologies can be negative, and self-destructive. No doubt they can be. They can also guide us to a noble death, a self-willed death, or a creative death. In every shadow prayer glimmers a light. In every prayer-light glooms a shadow.

In the end it always comes down to two questions: What do you pray for? And what will you do when your prayer is answered?

We must not allow ourselves to feel guilty about how we prayed, or what we remembered to pray or not to pray. Prayer guilt is a deadfall trigger against which souls may blunder on their way to spring.

We just finished working with a group of students at the university. Though it was late spring, the weather was rank that day they went out into the nature preserve to look for stories. What looked like a pleasant morning turned into a dark, wind-driven, rain-laced day. Poor folks. They bravely crossed the threshold and immediately started to look for ways of avoiding hypothermia. An intrepid few climbed to the heights, where they were numbed and flattened by the wind. Most of them dug in near the creek bed, where the gale didn't ruffle their feathers. We were glad for the ones who took whatever shelter they could find.

Later, when they had all returned and we were telling our stories in a frigid back room of the preserve, I realized how much prayer had existed that day. We had been praying like crazy to such unconventional spirits as oak, (in tree and poisonous form), creeks, moss, rocks, grass, wind, deer, flies, algae, swamps, wet boots, soaked socks . . . you name it.

Praying may not have made us any warmer. But it sure had given us some good stories to tell.

I can't pretend to be any kind of an authority on genetic memory. I think Sheldrake and the morphologists have a real case. That copse of willows in that particular spot down by the creek is remembering to be willow, growing in that particular fashion in that particular home. And that particular willow remembers both inside and outside itself. Its memory extends from the genetic structure of its cells outward into the space beyond itself. It co-occupies that space with many other species, is a host to some of them, and is parasitized by others. To some species the willow is a threat to their sun. To others, it provides neutral space in which there is no threat or predator. To a badger, it provides an extensive root system into which it can burrow and make its home. To a sparrow, it provides a nest. To a human—me—it provides welcome shade on a hot day. It also plays other roles with humans. It provides long, straight limbs for temporary bows and walking sticks, a certain bark from which can be made baskets or herbal tea, and the supports of temporary houses like wickiups and sweat lodges. I could go on. I think I see a tent caterpillar's nest up there.

I ain't no authority. I can only tell you what my memory says—that this copse of willows remembers everything that happens to it, and that this memory is passed on to its offspring who are even now poking up through the grass, rising from the seed-bed, remembering what happened last spring (and how many springs before), how much sun, how much rain, how much snow, how much wind, how much lightning, how many birds, how many bees, how many tent caterpillars, how many deer, how many humans.

Some might object and say that willows aren't that subtle. These same detractors would probably agree, however, that willows retain a genetic memory that goes back untold millions of years. So I'm wondering: if willows go back farther than humans, could they actually be as subtle, in their own way, as humans? How about more subtle? And if willows do indeed possess genetic memory, what exactly are the boundaries of this memory? Does it end at the bark? Does it end where the budding seed tears loose from the stem? Does it end where the fertile pollen-fluff fly to another clump of willows a quarter mile away?

If God created all things from memory, then all things must inherit the physical/psychological/rational/spiritual structure of God's memory. It might be that some have inherited more of this memory, some less, and that humans inherited some too.

I wonder how willows are reacting to pollutants in the air.

To tell you the truth, I wouldn't know where to put human "gifts" on a scale of one to ten. I think I'd give us a five, maybe a six. The long-term memory of humans is certainly no match for those mammals (bighorn sheep, dolphins, whales, wolves, lions, elephants, etc.) who seem to remember that the end is coming, and are ready to go off and die. Humans tend to hang on . . . and hang on—until death has to go through all kinds of gyrations to harvest us.

Death is the ultimate initiation. Like birth, it is the great determiner. In our death we vector by remembering. In our birth we vector by remembering. This determining is largely by memory—a simple, physical manifestation of God within us.

God-within me will determine. God the body, psyche, mind, and spirit within-me will determine.

How can we have the audacity to claim that this God within belongs only to homo sapiens? The whales remember with god-within-us. The jackrabbits remember with god-within-us. The magpies remember with god-within-us. The red dragonflies remember with god-within-us. All creation reverberates with the song of god-within-us!

EROS: FLIRTING, BEAUTY, MY WOMAN

We always say to our students, "Put eros on the wheel." In the summer you have erotic love, sensual love, sexual love—doesn't matter which gender. In the fall you have self-love, the dark quest of self-acceptance—doesn't matter which gender. In the winter you have love for others, love for family, spouse, community, friends, other species, the earth—doesn't matter which gender. And in the spring you have love for god, love for spirit, love for illumination, and love for the authoress of illumination (doesn't matter which gender).

Our culture tends to narrowly render eros as bodies rubbing against each other and all that delicious stuff. But eros is much more than that. Eros tugs at the soul, like the moon at the ocean, and always brings up feelings associated with the past.

Imaginary eros, remembered sex, touchings, feelings, emotions, ideas associated with the sexual act (doesn't matter which gender), compose a much greater womb in which eros can live. In this womb, the inward, psychological self gestates and blindly seeks to accept and know itself, even as it (so often) turns away from self in guilt or disgust.

Every act of sexuality goes into memory, even as the future flows through the passage of now into the past. We may not remember that one night stand—or maybe we remember it only too well—but juicy details are there for the taking if we should decide to go fishing.

Time has a way of eroding our ability to remember who, where, why, how, when we made love to someone who was very special. This maddening tendency, I fear, is nowhere more fully manifested than in my particular memory system. Indeed, my own tendency to forget erotic details has driven me to reexperience sexual love just to remember. Ah! That's what it is! I'm one of the worst of the forgetters. And my drive to remember is equal to my rate of forgetfulness.

Are you like me? If so, we must console each other. We may not be acutely aware of this tendency to forget, but it runs through us and all beings. I think whales, particularly dolphins, remember to forget better than we do. They are constantly rubbing and fondling—doesn't matter which gender—always trying to remember all over again HOW GOOD IT IS.

Usually, the greatest hindrance (therefore ally) to self-love is the opposite sex parent. Mama's boys. Daddy's girls. The anima and the animus. The inward eyes watching us, commenting on our behavior, loving us, judging us, ignoring us, manipulating us. Again and again, we have to go down into the arena of memory and duke it out. I am not the woman you see me as. I am not the man you raised me to be.

Rebel as wantonly as you will, and still you will not be free of those eyes. Finally in great weariness you give in. You make a compromise. You say, "I am not who you see me as. But I realize you are incapable of change. So I accept you as being that kind of mother or father, and in spite of the ways you raised me, I love you." This outflow of unmerited love to the parent invariably sets the rebel free. Well, not quite. Never quite free of those eyes. But free enough.

Put eros on the wheel and you come to the fall shield of self-love. Every apprentice in our program learns this. Erotic love begins with the desire for sensual gratification and passes through a very important developmental phase called adolescence where it is changed into "self-love." The attainment of self-love seems to require that we sever from childhood, that we love ourselves apart from our parents—that we see ourselves as essentially lovable.

Aye, there's the rub. Can you love yourself? Sometimes. Can I love myself? Sometimes. Don't ask me for the answer. I'm still trying to work this one out. Surely, after all those years and teachers of non-attachment and gurus false and true, I should not feel so ashamed about certain memories. But they haunt me. Time after time I summon the suddenly remembered woman, man or child and claim my complicity and ask for forgiveness. They forgive me. And I continue to wonder, "Is their willingness to forgive a gift from We Who Have Gone Before?"

❖❖❖❖

Self-love isn't easy to come by. I've been working at it for a long time. I don't think I'll have the problem licked by the time I kick the bucket. I tell myself that after I'm gone I'll have a long time to fall in love with my essential self.

Our inability to respect and accept ourselves seems to be a malaise of modern times. Our civilized childhoods provide us with plenty of memories to breed ants in our pants. We can't blame Mom and Dad any more than we can blame ourselves. We would probably have to go back to the hunter-gatherer phase to find human beings who were not tormented by memories of self worthlessness. Paul Shepard wanted to go back there. I want to go back there too. But it doesn't look possible. The best we can hope for are rites of passage in which our children can come to a fuller recognition of their own intrinsic worth, apart from their memories of childhood.

Woe betide us if we can't reach a more balanced view of our intrinsic worth, not only as individuals but as a species. The ways we project our self-disgust into our only home has undermined the foundations.

In the winter shield, we learn to love others by remembering how we have been loved. As we have been loved, so we love. And as we have not been loved, so we cannot love—or at least not without certain transformational experiences.

Parents love their kids partly because they hope that when the kids have their own kids, they will give them the same kind of love. Sometimes this love is all mixed up with do's and dont's and tainted with the struggle to love self.

We parents do our best. If it's not enough, then it's not enough. If it's too much, it's too much. If it's weird, it's weird. Parental love can get pretty crazy. But I suspect parents are not always quite as bad as they're hyped up to be on the psychiatrist's couch. Many children tend to get fussy around memories of the tit.

I vowed I would not love my children the way my parents loved me. Now that my children are grown I can see that I made some of the same mistakes my mother and father made—and some of my own. I could have done better. I could have done worse. But I do know, as my parents near death, that I love them all the more.

No doubt, much of what I did as an adult was influenced by memories of what my parents did or didn't do. To this day I continue to explore aspects of experience that were forbidden to me as a child. I had to know what I wasn't supposed to know. Now that memories of doing these forbidden things are stored in my head, I can see that, as with all cultural or familial taboos, the actual experience was no big deal. I wasn't struck down by lightning. I didn't go to hell. My outlook on life simply became a little bigger. With all my love, I wish this kind of growth for my children.

Wherever we go, we find the Devil. He is ubiquitous. It doesn't matter what we poke our nose into. We can find him in the church as easily as we can find him in the house of ill-repute. Memories of our own "sins" teach us tolerance and compassion. Memories of love teach us where to look for God. We can find him everywhere. It is easy to find him. God is love.

I know a young "tagger" who goes around spreading "graffiti art" on our public walls. He's been busted for it again and again, but he always goes back to it. He can't help it. He's no criminal. He's an artist. To tell him to stop tagging walls would be like asking him to stop breathing.

Some of us are born remembering that we are artists. And once that memory seizes us, we cannot forget. We remember until we die.

Every work of art is an act of memory. "SEMEN," this tagger calls himself. He spreads bold, bright, beautiful semen all over the city. You see it along the freeway. You see it on backyard fences, on benches in the park, on cinder block buildings, next to the entrance to the Bank of America. SEMEN, ejaculating his art into the concrete vulvas of the city.

"SEMEN" FERTILIZES WALL-EGG. OFFSPRING HALF-HUMAN, HALF-CONCRETE.

Art is no doubt among the highest of human callings. Artists must be allowed to die remembering who they are—because the Muses of Memory live within them. Through their lust to remember, these deities continually reinvent themselves in works of art.

Humans are no more exempt from creative lust than a flowering tree. Semen is still a teenager, a kid with a lousy father, without much of a home. But he knows what I'm talking about. Up and down his soul he's sprouting flowers. He knows it was God who left that come-spot on the wall.

Since teenage, I have truly enjoyed flirting with people. Didn't matter which sex. In the early days, flirting could lead to something more intimate. But now I am content to let flirting lead to nowhere but flirting.

Flirting has to be one of the higher callings—a vital legacy of the sacred ancestors. By flirting, we empower. And so our kind gives each other reasons to live another day.

Great things can never be accomplished without some kind of come-on. I can't believe that the Angel of the Lord who wrestled with Jacob was not, in fact, flirting with him. There must always be some kind of bait, some method of teasing, that brings out desire for the best in us. If we have a reason, no matter how titillating, to put our best foot forward, then why not?

If a god or goddess flirts with us, surely he or she is asking us to flirt back. Flirting always goes two ways. One goes towards the flirtee. The other goes towards the flirt.

People who profess to love Jesus and then proceed to do everything Jesus preached against forget that Jesus was a process as well. He wasn't exactly saying "love me if you want to live forever." He was saying, "love the process that gave birth to me and you will live forever."

We flirt with everything with which we come in contact. I remember my number one son, flirting with the willow trees in Vedauwoo, Wyoming, by hitting the branches with a stick, testing his strength against Willow. For all he knew, a rattlesnake might have been coiled at his feet. Flirting is jousting with a magic stick called Attraction. We assume that our environment is friendly, even when danger is nigh. So we test our erotic strength, innocently enough, against the other, hardly realizing it is the very source of our existence.

Attraction takes many forms, and every form can become a yoga, a means of attaining union with, and nurturing, Essence. Every yoga leads through the darkness to the light of reason, which brings us ultimately to the spiritual meaning for our tendency to flirt. Mother Earth is a flirt.

Perhaps at this very moment we are sitting alone on the sacred mountain of vision with an empty belly and no one to talk to. The noon sun thunders silently in the sky and everything has assumed a flat, shadowless aspect. The only sounds we hear are the monotonous buzzing of flies, the occasional call of an unseen bird. We wipe the sweat from our necks and try to appreciate the beauty around us. But our minds won't stay still. We find ourselves re-cycling through all-too-familiar territory, memories of times we were bored, depressed, suffering, when life seemed to cave in on us and nothing ever seemed resolvable.

We try to divert our attention from our troubles. We think, maybe I'll take a walk. Maybe I'll pick up my water bottle and take a swig. Maybe I'll find a cooler place. But we're too weak to move. We feel rooted to the ground, victims of circumstances we thought we were willing to endure. We look around with dull eyes. Is there anything out there that will divert our anger at ourselves for choosing to be here?

A nearby clump of sage sags under the full force of the heat. All day it has been struggling in the sun. Its leaves give off a burnt odor the American Indians consider sacred in their ceremonies. But for the moment we care little for this meager little bush. It looks like a thousand other clumps of sage bush. The sight of it only makes us feel worse. It reminds us of ourselves, growing up in an hostile, boring world, while karma presses us down, draining us of everything but hunger and thirst.

Is it not true that when we have come to this state of mind we are hardly capable of pronouncing our life beautiful? Beauty could be wafting the most exotic perfume into our nostrils but we are busily sniffing our own assholes.

My mother used to say, "Beauty is in the eye of the beholder." She was certainly on the right track. Beauty is reflected in the eye of the beholder. When we are receptive to beauty, beauty leaps for our eyes, like a lover. When we are wallowing deep in our own shit, shit splatters our eyes. Nature reflects back to us what we give to her. If we throw her a curve, she throws us a knuckle ball.

The wind is up today. The giant sequoia by the lake shudders and roars like a cataract. The cattails genuflect like acolytes in prayer. High in the whistling air, a red-tailed hawk rides a roller coaster of hunger, piercing the distance like a dart. Swifts skim the ruffled water for dragonflies. Is anything at rest today? Even my soul is agitated, tossed to and fro in the sky of summer like a shred of cottonwood fluff. I say to myself, "Be still. Wait. Let beauty come to you." But my memories will not comply. I am buffeted by the winds of the past.

It seems only yesterday I set out along the yellow brick road for the Emerald City. So young and fresh I was, so ready for the unknown. I spread my wings and gave myself to the hungry winds. "Take me to my destiny," I cried. We Who Had Gone Before knew where I was going, but they much preferred to let me discover for myself.

Many times I reached Oz. And many times I had to leave the Emerald City to vanquish the Wicked Witch of the West and her winged monkeys.

As I look back along the way, it seems the wind has eaten just about everything. But she didn't eat without leaving me grateful memories in exchange: of being blown down whenever I got too high on a ridge line; of the odor of lightning and the taste of fear; of dead ends and box canyons; of thunder-violent nights and sun naked days; of holding on for dear life and letting go; of children coming forth in the morning; of abjection, dereliction, stagnancy; ecstacy and exultation; love and care.

Now, as I round the last corner and see the sacred mountains hulking above me, I remember the wind filling the sails, the hissing wake, the curling foam, the cries of birds. Life is passion, ardor, verve, exhilaration, fervor. "Exuberance is beauty!" (Blake)

Considering the genetic fact that hundreds of billions of humans came together in the act of sexual memory to ultimately wind up with the sentient being that is me, I can claim without reservation that I am a long-time lover of human beauty.

At 18, I was fascinated by the "forbiddenness" of the unclothed body. I completely ignored any other quality that did not smack of lustful curiosity about what was under the clothes. Even now, I cannot underestimate the astonishment that an unadorned body can bring a magical erection.

Physical magic. I hardly ever considered the shadow of that attraction power—that the erection contained the even more mystical seeds of life. I just wanted to touch the beauty, to explore it with my eyes, to ease myself into it like a swimmer into a warm ocean.

Heedlessly, I made babies with my magical thing. Nature's plan was realized in the propagation of the species. She had birthed me so I could father children. A moment's dalliance, a lifetime of care!

Fatherhood brought its own appreciation of the beauty of women. In spite of my persisting lust for the mystery under the clothes, I came to love the inward beauty of the mother. I came to love her soul, her way of feeling, her way of dancing with exhaustion, routine, depression, and the constant demands of children. I loved how, after a working day, she would open herself to me in the ecstatic darkness of our bedroom. I even came to accept the hard beauty of her scorn, her fearful little girl, the sometimes maddening presence of her father, and her poignant need to fulfill, as deeply as I did, the meaning of her life.

From the perspective of elderhood, I can see how the early years of manhood were spent learning that beauty was more than skin deep. In middle age years I began to truly appreciate the beauty of my woman's mind. Even as the hard urges of the sexual drive softened, I learned the lessons of her intellect. She was not, as my culture had taught me, irrational, flighty, or unreasonable. Even when I fainted dead away in the arms of feeling, she could perceive the why, how, and angle of my fall. She had the power to discriminate between a blizzard and a flurry, a gale and a breeze. She steadied me, grounded me, awakened the full man in me. She yoked my mind to hers. We stood tall together, a force to be reckoned with. We became mother and father. Our children and grand-children prospered.

Almost before I knew it, I was an old man—and a fortunate one. For the love of beauty had never fled from me. Finally I was able to see the spirit of a woman—her likeness to the Goddess, her imagination, her faith, from whence came the word faith-full. I could acknowledge that this same spirit had come to dwell in me. When I touched the body of my beloved, I touched her with spirit fingers, the same fingers that had reached into my most holy places to bless me.

On the other side of the grave I will touch her beauty with these same knowing fingers.

Sometimes I kick myself for being one of the slow learners. Years passed while I languished in the doldrums of self-doubt. I could not bring my-self to approve the picture of my life I was painting. I kept thinking I could do better, even as the lines in my face multiplied, and my body sagged under the weight of years.

I could never have done better. And I could never have done worse. We Who Have Gone Before sang within me. They were not al-ways in tune, but the song painted the picture.

Their life work hangs before me, almost complete. The picture tells a story of the beauty of human nature.

I met her when she was 23, 13 years younger than I. At the time I was conducting a training class in death and dying for volunteers on the Marin County Suicide Prevention hotline. When I asked if someone would be willing to play dead, and to take a look at his or her former life from a coffin, only one person stepped forward. My woman.

She wasn't my woman then. She was someone else's woman. I had no idea that we would spend over 25 years of our lives together. To my way of thinking, she was an intelligent young person who had come forward to help me in my distress. I was impressed by her seriousness.

She said her father was gravely ill. Consequently she had been thinking about what it meant to die, for she was all too aware that death was everybody's portion. As the "corpse in the coffin," she spoke of her former life in terms of light and shadow, but there was nothing she regretted. Years later, she was to give herself a name, one of many self-namings that stuck: Lonely Heart Outreaching.

I didn't see her again for half a year, at least. And then my girlfriend at the time signed us both up for the training course in Suicide Prevention and Crisis Intervention. We agreed to attend together and maybe get qualified to serve on the hotline. The training course was rigorous, and my girlfriend worked on the other side of the Bay. It was easy for me to get to classes, much harder for her. She dropped out. I continued with the course, despite the fact that my particular way of observing the rules of "talking to suicidal people" was distressing my teachers.

When "invitation" time arrived (that is, being invited to serve on the hotline), I got a fervent lecture about listening carefully from the instructors and was told in no uncertain terms that if I was to accept an offer to serve on the hotline, I would have to partner with . . . . the woman who later became my partner for life.

I remained ignorant and unseeing. I thought my future involved my girlfriend and the insane relationship we had gotten ourselves into. I accepted the invitation, and began to serve with Meredith on the Thursday night suicide line.

When the phones blinked red, we picked them up. I did my best to hold my own with young Meredith, for I never would have made it without her. I seriously lacked the ability to listen really carefully to what the other person was saying. Meredith was one of the best. I listened to her talking on the phone and I learned just how far one had to go before one could earn a stranger's confidence, especially one who had swallowed pride and dialed the number of the very dread that loomed in his or her heart. Suicide! How carefully I had to listen!

It is one thing to sift for alternatives. It is another thing to listen. I was good at the first. I was a beginner in the second. So I listened to M, and now, after 25 years of listening, I can see how much I have to learn.

A lifelong love is composed of many ingredients. One of them is the desire to learn from the other, and a great respect for the teacher, even when the lesson is hard, damn hard.

❖❖❖❖

Not that my woman is without her weaknesses, or that I am a fanatical worshipper at the shrine. There are ways I can teach her too, and there are learning times for her, even when she doesn't realize it at the moment. I'd say we are pretty much evenly matched.

Evenly matched ego-wise. We are only human. Sometimes I detest her. Sometimes she is so sick of me she could vomit. Being "evenly-matched" means that now and then you get so fed up you want nothing more than to get the hell out of there. Ah, love. But then again there are those times when we stand in awe of each other's presence.

A battle, yes, at least sometimes. A winner, never. And most of the time the sounds of warfare are so far away you'd swear the front lines didn't exist. Love means letting each other down. Love means being unthinkingly stepped on. Love means taking the anger full on and not owning it, at least all of it. Love means sleepless nights of tossing and turning because you are not feeling close even though you want to be. Love is sometimes not turning and tossing because you are close again. Love is remembering what you said, and regretting it, and trying to think of reasons why you said it in the first place. Love is thinking back on all the ways she/he was there for you.

Love is a dark hole. Love is a mountain shining in the distance. Love is now, when I am so pissed at you I won't speak for a year. Love is being at a loss for words because the other is weeping because she feels so much. Love is a prayer we keep praying even when we are not kneeling at the altar. Love persists, and not simply because love takes us into her arms and sets us down with our feet on the earth. *Love persists.*

Love must have my assent and your assent. Usually, it is the simplest act that makes the difference. We open up the door, thinking our wrists are too feeble to twist the knob. Then love comes rushing in.

When all is said and done, love is not nostalgic. Sure, we've always had good times together. But what's this? Do I have to go through this all over again? Love keeps jumping up to face the challenge. As we get older, we don't face fewer challenges. The mountains get bigger. The holes get deeper.

And gradually we have learned to keep our balance a little better. We see those bottomless pits ahead of time, and so we can more often avoid them.

All those years I've been travelling a road leading to a woman I hardly even know. We've slept together for 25 years or so. Rarely were we ever apart. We have each other's habits down to a T. We know what the other is going to say before we open our mouths. But just today I watched her walk out of the trees and I thought, who is this stranger? She stands so beautifully, even as I sink into wrinkles. Why doesn't she grow old, like me? Why, she's the same girl I married 25 years ago!

❖❖❖❖

She leaves a note on my desk while I am away in the desert. It says, "You are my sweet love, full of dark chocolate and rainbow colors. Your Honey." Sentimental, eh?

She sits on the floor, massaging our daughter, who, halfway through her senior project at college, has come to hang out at home. Mother and daughter make quite a pair, talking about relationship, while the TV news personality reads cue cards about the latest atrocity in L.A.

She sits beside me in a circle of students. She is talking about rattlesnakes, how to anticipate and avoid them in the desert. In two days we will take these people into the Mojave where they will live alone for four days and nights without any food or shelter. The students bend forward so as not to miss a single word. She knows what she is talking about.

She comes into the house from the upper orchard. Her face is flushed as if she has just had sex. Actually, she has been pruning the apple trees and raking the leaves from the grass. Who would know the difference? Certainly not me. Immediately I am suspicious, jealous. An elf has gotten into her pants.

She hunches over her desk, hand-writing the tenth letter today, the hundredth this week, each one penned with empathy and care. Dear So and So. I loved your letter. How was your operation for colon cancer? Have you seen your daughter lately? What are your plans for the coming year? No, unfortunately, that course is filled, but we can put you on a waiting list. Stay in touch. Love.

She goes to the post office and winds up talking with half a dozen townsfolk on her way home. It's not gossip she's after. She just wants to give people a chance to talk about what's on their minds. A local healer?

She dresses in manlike clothes and doesn't wear makeup except around her eyes. Sometimes people mistake her for a pretty boy and look at me with a certain curiosity. There's something outrageous about the way we appear together—I, the aging, gray-haired man, she the youthful figure in jeans and sport coat, the blue arrowhead dangling from her ear. We hang out and watch people. We don't have to say much. A glance between us says it all.

I can see her now. She walks like a little girl, her long legs reaching out, her arms swinging free. I can't keep up with her any more. I turned around and she was gone, a dot in the distance, a bit of milkweed fluff riding on the wind.

She's out in the desert watching over the group while I come home to rest. The house is empty without her. I can't reach the public radio station. No one sits in the big chair by the front window cracking sunflower seeds between her teeth and reading romantic novels. When I open the refrigerator, all I can find is food she left for me.

She turns into my back and hugs my shoulder. Just a moment ago, her hips were moving beneath mine, her eyes glazed over, forehead wrinkled in concentration. Oh, sweet Jesus, she kissed my neck!

All these memories, dearest heart, I commit to you.

I think M has "made" me. That is, she has seen where I wanted to go and then did everything she could to help me get there. I think I have done the same for her, but I think it was much easier for her to help me make myself than for me to help her make M. I was the eldest of four children within five years of age, and I had to scrabble and spit to maintain my place in the hierarchy. Raised in a divorced family of ten (twice as many kids as in mine), M always seemed to know her place, even when she was drastically tested by the emergencies and tragedies of her life. She was, in the jargon of the culture, centered, grounded, rooted, self-assured. And I, battered I, was always happy to be the moth circling the hearth flame.

This ability to hold her ground and see who I was trying to be, is the mark of genius. M can't spell worth a damn (she's getting better!) but she can spell another person very well, thank you. She is best at spelling her man—and her children.

Am I talking about some kind of ideal woman-wife-lover mother? Why, just the other day she refused to acknowledge my existence. Why? Don't be ridiculous. She's not perfect.

Selene Foster: Ink and graphite on paper, '99

YOUTH AND POETRY

Thirty years have passed since we first began to take young people into the wilderness to fast for three days and nights to confirm their attainment of maturity—and the magic of rites of passage remains. If anything, it's stronger. Only today, a group of young adults told their threshold stories to assembled parents and elders and tearfully took leave of Lost Borders. Nobody was shedding more tears than this old man.

Once again the inescapable truth is driven home. The young know where it's at. They are drawn like flies to the eternal truths of human experience. Love is God and God is love. A 17-year-old girl knows this better than most so-called adults. She may not be schooled in the finer points of experience, but she remembers very well, and has acquired the intellectual apparatus to speak in the most profound ways.

This afternoon we listened in council to the story of this same young woman, a freshman at U.C. Santa Cruz, who had just returned from a three day and night solo fast in the Inyo Mountains. She had written a letter to her mother, a Polish Jew from the labor camps of Russia who lost half her family in the Warsaw ghetto.

"Dear Mom,

There are some things I would like to tell you. I am aware of the sacrifices you have made for your family. I know you dropped everything you know and who you are to provide what you thought was best for your loved ones. You have endured countless hardships, no doubt, and have denied love for yourself in the process. It could not have been very easy when not only did you find yourself a stranger in an unwelcoming land, but also a stranger in your own house.

I have spent many years rejecting your lifestyle and pushing you away. Because that was all I knew of you, that was all I lived to judge and I judged harshly too often. I would like now to extend the invitation to know you and for you to know me, because we have changed and existing impressions are no longer accurate. I am ready to accept who you are if you can accept who I am, but guards need to be let down and willingness needs to be the foundation. Love always falls in the footsteps of acceptance. I am ready to listen and accept.

I am so sorry for the hurt I have caused, because love and acceptance are virtues that should always be found in your blood when the rest of the world seems to fall. Believe me, I am scared too.

Love,
A."

In this age when the old rites of passage have been forgotten or ignored or even considered "wicked," the young have been forced to create their own rites. After all, the acceptable ways of becoming "adult" are pretty boring—like the driver's license, the credit card, high school graduation, the 21st birthday. What is there for a "teenager" to do if the growth event is not ultimately related to the attainment of mature insight? Is it not true that the finest of our youth are deeply attracted by experiences that test them so that they can "know?"

I can't help but go back to the 60s and 70s of the last century. The kids were going crazy, smoking weed and dropping acid and getting high on speed. We threw up our hands in despair. What shall we do with our young? Did we decide collectively (with the aid of our legal system) to shut them down, to wage war against them, to make them pay for their transgressions so that they could see straight? The young of this generation are paying for our inability to see them.

Forty years ago, a certain cultural event occurred which could never be undone. The young had made a statement, and it would only be a matter of time before some other youthful generation went "crazy" in a similar way—and again the subject of revolution would rear its ugly head.

As long as we deny our youth any kind of "real initiation" (at least to them), we will face the inevitability of revolution. The reasons are quite obvious. Those who have authority over us have never attained adulthood. They have forgotten the old rites of passage. Holy Shit! The chariots are rumbling into battle and there is nobody in them but bullets and bombs!

We are ignoring the tragic lessons learned by We Who Have Gone Before.

The young are all in search of stories. "My story." Do the parents want to impose their own stories on them? This is idiocy, and will lead to revolution and chaos. The children must be given a chance to inherit their own stories. If we are to survive, the stories must all, in one way or another, be about how we came to love and understand ourselves, our earthly environment and our places upon it. We must give them the most mature chance we can imagine for them. All we have to do is listen to the stories of We Who Have Gone Before.

Will we listen? At the beginning of the next century, it doesn't appear so.

Those of us who attempt in our own ways to "anchor" our communities may not be able to recognize the ways in which the youth pursue that elusive and magnificent ideal of Love. They seem, in fact, to be going in the opposite direction. We forget how we went about it. We forget to listen to the wisdom of our own memories. We forget how alienated, how lonely, how uncertain we were—as we were setting forth into a future that did not seem to comprehend or care about what we were trying to do. Some of us survived this passage. Others succumbed to self-pity. Most care little one way or the other. Into this ocean of ambivalence a candidate for President of the United States drops, like a minor disturbance. He says he understands what the youth are saying. But few of the youth are voting.

What is it that youth really want? Surely the candidate for President has no idea, or if he does, he would never dare to put it into practice. The youth want Love. They want to experience and talk about it. They want to grow up into Love. Can't he hear them dancing and shouting and carrying on? All is in turmoil. The rigid and the morally unforgiving are trying to control the foreverness of the young, who hunger, like We Who Have Gone Before, for rites of passage into the regions of Love.

The law denies the young the approbation of their community. The law does not speak for the whole community, and merely tries to correct. The law knows not love. If neighborhoods were tribes—and they are—the tribe itself would deal with the intractable youth, and find ways to correct by nature and nurture. The tribe itself, in which the local school plays only a part, would help the young find a story and a calling to match the restless wandering of their hearts.

The law will not allow this wandering to be. For every offense there must be a corresponding punishment. Hence, the law conditions the tribe to treat the young as criminals, and to cheer when the punishment is meted out. Thus treated, the "criminal" young never receive the nurturing of their tribal community. They are cut off from empowerment and hope. They are doomed to carry the scar of an outcast through their adult lives, and can only "heal" themselves by learning to become what the law wants them to be.

Some learn. Many don't. If the way of blame and punishment is the only way to reach adulthood, then we will all suffer the consequences of this kind of "correction." Either we will continue to rebel against unreasonable authority (and continue to be punished), or we will become hypocritical adults, hiding our rebellion until the hidden wanderlust all but vanishes, and we too are enslaved by the Law.

Long ago, when my wife and I were falling in love, we decided to take a group of 28 adjudicated youth on a crazy hippie bus trip to *Baja California Sur* for $50 apiece. It was a foolhardy adventure. The bus broke down; our support vehicle, a jeep, became mired in the mud flats of *Bahia Concepción*; two underage girls mutinied and disappeared into the Mexican night; and we ran out of money 1,200 miles below the border. Certain kids came forward to take leadership roles in this crisis, among them a beautiful young woman we called Spotted Fawn.

There was a quiet competence and unearthly grace in Spotted Fawn, an unflappable optimism, a deep interest in what was going on around her. She never lost her cool, even when a couple of rape-minded Mexican men appeared in a battered Ford with pistolas jammed into their belts. I can clearly remember her response to this threat. While some of her girlfriends strutted around in their halter tops, she went inside the stranded bus and put on a shapeless t-shirt. She stood beside us as M and I held our ground and hinted about the men with bigger pistolas than theirs who were coming back to join us momentarily. The thugs backed off and drove away, shooting their guns harmlessly into the air.

Five years later, Spotted Fawn, a sophomore at Humbolt State University, was hitching back to college on Highway 101, and was picked up by a serial killer. The man tied her to a tree, tried unsuccessfully to rape her, and killed her with a shotgun.

Spotted Fawn has lived with me since then. She haunts my dreams. The only way I can find peace with her is to realize that while she was undergoing this fatal ordeal she was keeping her cool, and remembering how to die, and that while she was in the death passage the sacred ancestors told her where to go.

I define myself as a writer. I often wonder if that's the right thing, but there's simply nothing I can do about it. I am compelled to write—and then to dislike what I have written. I know I'm not the only writer who feels this way. But I do tend to wonder why it is that I indulge myself in such a hopeless task.

Even as a high school jock, I had to give vent to whatever I was feeling or thinking. This compulsion (ancestral memory?) to create and then tear down what has been built, has always made me feel separate from most other humans.

And now I see the same tendencies in my daughter, who has just graduated from college with a major in art. Like her father, she is never quite satisfied with what she has done. There is no turning back for her either. This art stuff is woven into the very fiber of her being. She's not going to come to a crossroads someday and leave the artist behind. Both of us have been bitten by the same kind of snake, and the only antidote is a river running down to the sea. There is only one way to go—the way of We Who Have Gone Before.

What could we be remembering? Why would Mother Nature have created such a despairing, longing memory in humans? Is it that she thinks of us as she does of plants and trees, that she is reminding us to flower, and to bear fruit?

The more we think about it, the more we see within all nature the longing to be a poem.

Most definitions of poetry are too limited. Humans don't create poetry, nature does. Humans are merely recording machines, translators, wind harps. All other natural beings play the same role. Nature sings poetry through us. I watch our once wild dog cavort down by the lake. My tongue alone can never express the grace she is singing. I feel a moment of intense frustration, then relax. Let the dog be dog, for godsake. Don't write a poem about dog. Watch Dog!

According to Greek myth there was a presumptuous young man, Thamyris, who challenged the Muses to a poetry contest. He failed miserably. Nature's handmaidens paid him back for his impudence by blinding him and breaking his harp into a thousand pieces.

Who among us is so callused as to forget nature's expression of poetry and song? Sometimes the narrow-mindedness of certain scientists drives me crazy. They say: "Nature does not harbor such fuzzy sentiments as a love for beauty." Then why does the human species love beauty?

The impudence of Thamyris was the impudence of a slob. He belittled the poetry of nature. "What is wind but an objective term?" he said.

Nature broke his harp.

"It seems complicated, but it isn't," I remember my college literature teacher telling us. "Instead of saying something is *like* something else, you say it is something else." He gave several examples gleaned from the poems we were studying. "Time is an ocean." "A river is a road." "A kingfisher is a flame." "Stars are candles." I understood immediately what he was talking about. In the mirror of language, everything reflected everything else. Nothing stood alone and apart. Everything blended together; everything was a metaphor for everything else.

In the crassness of my sophomore year, I began to understand the nature of magic. Late at night, while my roommates were asleep, I read poetry under the candle lamp above my desk and saw how all things in nature changed their shapes into other shapes, how an orange changed into a ball, a leaf into a finger, an earthworm into a drill, a cactus into a spider web, a feather into a balloon, a seed into a garden. Nothing, absolutely nothing, seemed to stay the same. I looked up from my reading into the flickering shadows on the ceiling—light wavering into shadow, and shadow into light.

Meta means change, movement from here to there, transference. *Phore* means "bearer." *Metaphore*: "bearer of change."

Dear students of mine. How do we shift the shape of things to come? We transfer, we bear. We take "me" and convey it to "Nature." We take "war" and bear it to "peace." We take "desert" and change it to "rain." We take "sorrow" and transfer it to "joy." We take "hopelessness" and carry it all the way to "faith."

Follow me to the deepest, most mysterious metaphor of all: "Death is birth. Birth is death."

Don't tell me you know the difference between the two. I won't believe you. Nature shows no inclination to forget they are interchangeable. If birth and death were not one and the same, then we would certainly not be here. Life as we know it would either be one or the other. This, of course, is impossible.

Back and forth, the morphogenetic seesaw totters. Too heavy on one end? Not to worry. Soon there will be a shift to the other end. Birth means everything but death. And death means everything but birth. If you tell me you know which "everything" is which, I'll take you for a fool. I have no idea where I'm going.

> The breath of [memory] moves through a
> deathless valley
> Of mysterious motherhood
> Which conceives and bears the universal seed,
> The seeming of a world never to end,
> Breath for men to draw from as they will:
> And the more they take of it, the more remains.
>
> —Lao Tzu, *The Tao*

What is not and what is. Metaphor conveys what is to what is not. In so doing, metaphor makes "what is not" "*what is.*" This is no facile conundrum. It's a basic fact of our existence, of the eons of memory stored within the present. If we do not have access to what is not, we will never be able to use what is. And *vice versa.*

Metaphor: an inward way of seeing that leads into the outer world.

Metaphor: an outer way of seeing that leads into the inner world.

> Emptiness is fullness.
> Fullness is emptiness.
> The use of clay in molding pitchers
> Comes from the hollow of its absence.
>
> —Lao Tzu, *The Tao*

Enantiodromia. The dramatic tension between opposites. Metaphor. This is that and that is this. Not *like. Is.* East is west and west is east. The other name for light is dark.

Grandmother, teach me this mystery. Lead me to the Great Tension. Cut off my arms and legs and head. Make me dwell there, in the riptide, like a nameless creature of the tide pools rooted to the slimy rock of metaphor.

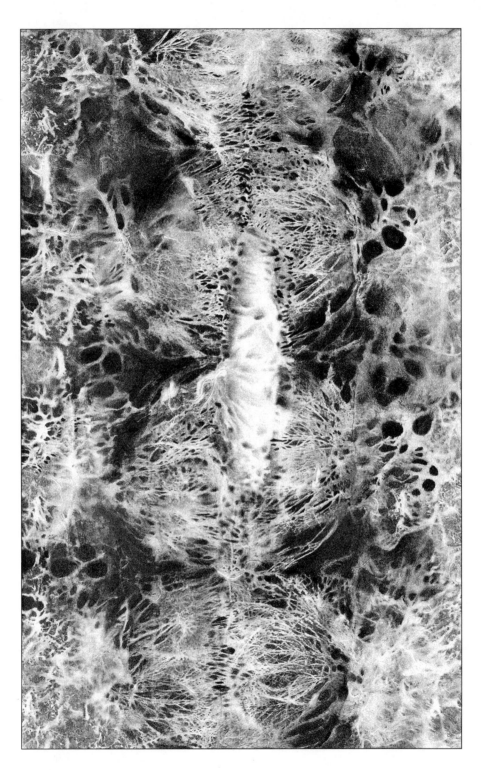

Selene Foster: Photo transfer and graphite on rice paper, '99

Synapses and Roads

I asked a neurosurgeon what memory meant to him. He thought awhile, then said, "synapse." When I asked him what he meant by that, he said, "Sensory experience is carried to the brain by synapses."

So I looked up "synapse" in the dictionary. The word is formed by two words—"syn" ("together") and "apsis" ("a joining"), and is psycho-neurologically defined as "a connection point between two neurons, where nerve impulses are transmitted from one to the other."

There must be a million of these connection points between the body and the psyche, tiny/vast bridges that convey the here and now of the physical world into the remembered events stored in the brain that compose the psyche. Passages between now and yesterday, between here and then/there.

I like the idea of synapse. Conveyer, passage, bridge, connector, spanner, co-relator—*metaphore*. Something that connects Point A with Point B. If Point A is the present moment, then Point B is tomorrow.

What I experience now I will remember tomorrow. That is, I will remember the anticipated future as happening yesterday—so that I can remember the past tomorrow.

Every day, every hour, every second we brave that fantastic journey into tomorrow, we remember it yesterday.

Perhaps we die when the tomorrow of death becomes the memory of birth.

Cling to a simple trust in the synapse. To get from Point A to Point B we have to cross the synapse, the boundary between body and soul. We have to cross this synapse because our body must connect to memory or it will not survive.

The border between body and soul is a labyrinth, a threshing hold, a switching yard, in which the experiential body is processed, sorted, and sent into memory. The body stays more or less intact, however, until it finally has to give itself away completely to memory.

The lost border between body and psyche interests me. I've given the better half of my life to studying it, as an initiate and as an initiatory midwife. Long ago, our sacred ancestors remembered that the border was actually a threshold world, a twisting passageway in which the sensations of the body lost their physicality and became the invisible stuff of feeling and thought. They considered the border to be a kind of testing ground, ingress to higher and higher stages of maturity. They exploited it. They sent their kids into it. They themselves walked that sacred path. They cultivated the synapse between the present and the past. They knew that if this bridge, this proving ground, was lost, they, as a people, were lost.

After thousands of years, the border was, in fact, lost. The rites of passage between body and soul fell into disrepair. Now our bodies grope for our souls like rain in parched ground. We have fallen unconscious. We have forgotten. And what we have not forgotten, we sleepwalk.

What keeps us from remembering?

Yesterday I ate something and got "food poisoning." All of a sudden I became dizzy; sweat broke out over my skin; my eyes wouldn't focus properly; I needed desperately to relieve myself of the contents of my stomach. I knew I had been invaded by something that could kill me, and reacted appropriately.

How did I know? My body remembered that an invasion had occurred—and my body acted to expel the poison. Did I egotistically "remember?" No. This kind of memory runs far deeper than "I." "Sickness," my ages-old body said to itself. But the exchange between body and memory was already occurring. Healing impulses had already been sent to the entire system: "Danger! Repel invader!"

I ran for the bathroom. The food leapt from my stomach like a stone from a sling. What splashed into the bowl was brought into the light of day by We Who Had Gone Before.

Automatically, we trust the synapse. After all, it is so ancient in us. The body memory connection seems to go back to the beginning of life itself. We humans are but an infinitesimal part of it.

Who or what remembered to give us that connection? Scientists say there is no god. Then they lose themselves in the wonder and mystery of the body. Why should memory be any different than god?

This ability to remember to react to the presence of poison, however, is more than genetics. The psyche remembers, and the mind, which can identify the name of the invader, also remembers. The spirit remembers too. From where else comes the impulse to heal?

Is life itself merely physical matter seeking to survive, perpetuate itself, and evolve? Is life more than just physical body?

Sometimes the poison that enters the system is extremely subtle. The invader can be disguised as something else. It can trick the memory with a frontal assault, only to slip in the back door. It can be odorless, colorless, tasteless, common. Subtle poisons can and do kill, sometimes slowly. No doubt they are concocted by memory itself, for we also know that all life must die.

One of the subtlest poisons is addiction. He tried it once. It was groovy. He decided to try it again. It was great. He tried it again. It wasn't half bad. He tried it again, to rescue the original feeling it had given him. The feeling wasn't quite like the first time, but it was good enough to make him try again. He was hooked. The poison was in him; it was killing him; and still he kept remembering how good it felt.

If the addict does not remember soon enough that the poison can kill him, then he will fall victim to the wrong memory. It's like Bonnie and Clyde remembering that they could very well die in a hail of bullets, then irrationally kicking back in the heat of the chase to make love.

Poison memories take advantage of the ways survival memories can play us false. The addict who labors under the misconception that poison is good for him has lost contact with a basic truth of life. If he would remember well enough, he would get a vaccination. But he doesn't remember well enough. Memory distracts him with another memory— pleasure. He embraces the pleasure, only to be killed by the poison.

Who says nature is benign? The memory banks of nature seem to be imbued with a dynamic tension between life-engendering actions and deathwarding actions—memories that are true to life and memories that are true to death. And we puny humans have to walk into that tension and sort out the truth from the lie. We have to walk into the synapse, where the present becomes past, where the body becomes soul—and where memory is lord of all.

Our friend Jed has some kind of creature in his gut, and his body doesn't like it. He picked it up in India years ago. The doctors tell him this and that and give him all kinds of medication, but nothing seems to work. The creature won't be identified. And his immune system seems to have forgotten what to do in the event it was invaded by the beastie.

The thing doesn't kill him. But it makes him so acutely uncomfortable he wishes he were dead. Imagine having a tapeworm slithering around in your intestines and none of the experts can tell you what it is. If you don't know what it is, you can't get rid of it. Identification is absolutely essential. Oh, it's a rat. I'll set a trap for it.

On the other hand, you could describe Jed's condition as an alien invasion. An unidentified life form landed in his gut and decided to stay there, finding in this "atmosphere" the necessary ingredients for survival. Looking around at what was provided, the creature decided not to conquer this world, but to live in it as a parasite. That was fine for the alien. Not so good for the host planet.

The beings native to the host planet were forced to adapt to the invader. In some cases, they succeeded. In others, they failed—or they malfunctioned. Others ran to help, and were caught up in the drama. Somehow, the host planet continued to exist. Crippled, it searched its memory banks for information about the invader. Information was sketchy. There was a complex of causes. So the host planet remembered to integrate the alien into its being.

An heroic Jed persists in living a strong, good, loving life, rising every morning with a subtle poison in his gut. Every day he goes to the wailing wall and prays to remember what manner of creature landed on his planet. Every night he sets traps for it, cunning things devised to catch the most hideous monsters.

God remembers. But God ain't telling. God is playing a memory trick on Jed. Why, in the infinite mercy of his memory, would God withhold the healing cure?

Why was Job visited with boils? Why was Jonah swallowed by a whale? Why was Jesus nailed to a tree?

We Who Have Gone Before remember that there must be men and women in the midst of us, heroes and heroines—marked ones—who take on the medicine power of subtle poisons. Their ability to survive in the shadows must never be quite understood. We who live on the host planet are depending on unanswerable questions.

I just drove down Highway 395 from Reno. I've driven that road a hundred times, and always, the beauty of the Eastern Sierra takes my breath away. I think I've memorized every curve, every straightaway, every town, every crossroad. If I want to pass someone, I already know if the double line ahead becomes broken, or vice versa. I'm pretty sure I can negotiate the road more safely than a stranger can.

But familiarity breeds contempt. I could become over confident or absentminded, and forget a 35 mph turn, or not allow for the sudden appearance of unanticipated danger—a deer crossing the road, an accident at a blind curve.

Same thing happens on the road of life. We think we know where we're going. But no matter how well memory serves us, it doesn't anticipate chance, overconfidence, or forgetfulness. Nevertheless, despite all possible happenstance, we walk the memory road, come what may.

Memory has its flaws. It can only be an accurate predictor. But beyond prediction lies the real tomorrow—the next hour, the next second. Memory can only say, "Maybe it will happen. Maybe not."

I'm just a frail and fatuous fool, still trying to learn that what happened was supposed to happen.

Road. The Yellow Brick Road that leads to Oz and the Emerald City. And when we finally reach Oz we discover that the Wizard is nothing more than a slight-of-hand man, that brains are nothing but pins and needles, that hearts are nothing but silk stuffed with sawdust, and courage nothing more than something we drink.

If that's all it is, why are people always trying to get ahead of us on this road to the Emerald City? Why are they so hasty to learn that it was all fake, that nothing was what it seemed? They blink their lights and honk their horns and get right up on your butt. Move over, they scream, and go roaring past like hell bent on destruction.

Is death the fulfillment of our dreams? Is that why folks are trying so hard to get ahead? Or is death merely another Emerald City along the way?

Migratory paths are roads predicated on the will to survive—which makes them clear and determined. These ancient species paths are so very precise because the incredible journeys are always undertaken across the Land of Death. The Mayas and Egyptians were quite specific about this fact. The Map of Life is drawn through the Underworld.

Death is the great Cartographer-in-Absentia, the hidden design behind the life path. No doubt that's why the aborigines drew pictures of song lines and migratory synapses upon obdurate stone. The old ways, the trails, the habits, the means of survival had to be passed on. The young always had to know. There must always be a trail leading to the place where the children are born. There IS a way through the underworld.

If you are yearning to travel, pick up something, anything, and look into it. Not at it—into it. Suddenly you will be on a road going somewhere. All you have to do is ask the map where it came from.

We are all travelers on this road called Where Do You Come From. But just when we think we know where it (whatever it is) originated, we have to ask the question again.

Where Do You Come From goes a long, long way back. How far back? So far back we wind up in the Future. So you could say that the road called Where Do We Come From is the synapse called Where Are We Going.

Torment and Flowers

Like most every one else, I have been tormented by memories. Most of my tormenters are not violent or traumatic. I often wonder why I have been spared violence.

How about you? Are you the one out of every four who has been mugged, raped, shot, stabbed, brutalized, hit by a drunk, shattered in a car crash, wounded in a war, blasted by a tornado, fried by a volcano, engulfed by a flood . . . ? If so, you have suffered at one time or another from post-traumatic stress.

Post-traumatic stress is caused by remembering. Suddenly the awful memory over-shadows consciousness like a predatory bird. You can't run and hide. Once again you must suffer yourself to be gripped by the talons of the past. You must relive the event, in gory detail.

Needless to say, memories such as these don't do much to enhance self-confidence, or balance, or a dispassionate view of the world, and have a way of ruining relationships. Such memories are like wounds that tear open just when you think the skin has knitted over.

You can see how trees remember traumatic events, how they grow twisted, curved, inverted, gnarled, diseased. Decades of wind and frost and snow and lightning and searing heat and parasitical invasion have taken their toll. Their tortured shapes are literally memories made visible. We say, "That tree has character."

"Character" is just another metaphor for soul. Those memories that torment us are molding our souls. They may come unbidden and force us, no matter how reluctantly, to relive the event, to feel victimized, angry, ashamed, despairing. But they define, shape, and grow us. They can even give us power—power to see into lies, power to act in the name of value and truth.

I'm no New Age airy fairy. Life is not all sweetness and light. A wound is a wound. The tormentors are leeches. You pull them off bloated with your life blood. But if you open your veins to them, you're a goner.

Everybody knows this—even the most primitive of castaways living on the megalomaniacal Human Survival Island.

I know a man who, as a youngster, was raped repeatedly by a drunken father until he left home. The man is now a successful superior court judge. But there are nights when he wakes up in bed drenched with sweat, tormented with anger and self-loathing. He has never forgotten those nightmares. He lives with them, and his wife and three children. Every day, as he makes rulings concerning the future of abused and forgotten children, he relives the horrors of his own childhood. He sits in the palace of Blind Justice.

A memory can pump us up or drain us. It all seems to depend on how we choose to remember. If I am depressed, I may choose to remember events in a negative way. For example, after a fight with M, I usually treat myself to a plate of dark memories—of times when I fought with her, or with other women, or with other people in general. In these dark orgies, I often see myself as the bad guy or the fool.

I often wonder why I actually cultivate memories that rob me of enlightened vitality. It's not that I haven't had the chance to become illuminated. I've opened my veins to a lot of leeches and lost a lot of borders. I've hit rock bottom so many times I should have tied a pillow to my ass. But I've also walked godlike on the land and shivered in the power of the spirit. You say, all I have to do is get saved? Well, I've been saved a hundred times, brother. And still I have this problem. Why do I keep on defeating myself in such asinine ways?

Do you think I'll make it to the streets of gold?

"No," say the Buddhists, "But you can make it to Nirvana. Just practice non-attachment."

I would, if I weren't so glued to love karma. Wife, children, grandchildren, friends, work, gardens, home, people who come to visit, the ringing phone, the IRS—not to mention my shady past and all its associated memories. I guess I wouldn't be a very good candidate for Buddhahood.

Looks like I'll have to go around again. Maybe next time I'll be born into a body ready for even more difficult challenges.

Ah life. This afternoon, while driving back from one of the most beautiful places in the Inyo Mountains, I tormented myself with memories. In this case, they were memories of people I fancied I had snubbed or let down. I must have entertained myself with feelings of shame and regret for a half an hour or so.

Meanwhile the road, bordered on each side by blooming rabbit brush, unwound beneath the humming wheels. Even as I harbored my dark thoughts, the golden blooms were loving my eyes. Kiss, kiss, kiss, the sensuous roadside nuzzled past. And all the while I was thinking about what I had done to other people, how I wished I had done otherwise.

Finally, just as the road settled into the deep valley in which we live, I asked out loud for forgiveness from everyone. "I'm sorry," I said to the windshield of the Cruiser. "I am who I am. I can be no other." Instantly, the valley arose to meet my eyes. Such a beautiful, magnificent home!

Life is so good.

❖❖❖

The word, flower, is one of those magical nouns that serve as a metaphor for all kinds of things. The universe is a flower. Her smile is a flower. Dawn is a flower. The book is a flower. Hope is a flower. Among the more apt metaphors are those pertaining to sensuality/sexuality. The penis is a flower. The vagina is a flower. The buttocks are flowers. The flesh is a flower. Lips and eyes are flowers. Opening thighs are flowers. Fingers are flowers. Orgasm blooms like a flower. And so on.

The dictionary of word origins says that the word flower comes from the Latin, *fluores*, which is also the root of the English term *menses*. It all makes sense when one realizes that the flower is the reproductive organ of the plant world. In time and season, the plant makes itself ready for orgasm by making flowers. Even so, for the woman coming into season, florescence is at hand. The pistil will soon be ready to receive the stamen.

One cannot escape the romantic connotations of this metaphor. The flower means reproduction. The flower is eros. To this day, when you fly to Hawaii, you are greeted with a necklace of flowers. "Aloha!" the natives say, and embrace you. You have travelled across the great sea to the islands of flowers. Eyes are laughing, bodies are willing. The sun shines down like a lover's eye; the scent of blooming hangs heavily on the air.

M and Gigi cut bunches of perfect roses and bring them into the house. The dining room air is heavy with the scent of red and white. "We love you," they are saying to me. My eyes are full of tears. When I die, will someone bring me flowers?

Flowers have a room of their own in the great mansion of ancestral memory. All we need to do is open the door. Come with me to the room marked "Flowers." Turn the handle.

In Norman Spinrad's classic science fiction novel, *Child of Fortune*, the heroine, a young girl, finds herself in the middle of the Bloomenvelt, a vast interconnected forest complex of flowers on an alien planet. Marooned without food, she realizes that she will have to survive on the blossoming fruit to find her way out. The only way to know if the fruits are beneficial—or deadly poison—is by experimentation.

The heroine moves through this alien-earth jungle toward the realization of her destiny. She undergoes the rites of the flower passage. She emerges as the "Pied Piper of the Bloomenvelt."

The stem droops, the leaves wilt, the flower twists into a dry caricature of its former self. The colors fade, the sepal dries, the ovary shrinks and draws in upon the gestating seeds. The whole dies to make seeds. All of life has been given to that final maturation.

The seed drops from the mother, is caught by the air and carried to the receptive soil, where winter freezes it into a death-like trance. But this simulation of death is ephemeral. The seed-life is quickened; a new flower comes forth.

Why should we think life is any different for us? Why should we think our blooming will last forever? Winter always comes. And so does spring.

The Calling and Forgetting

I know a woman who, from the time she was young, had been told by We Who Have Gone Before what she had been put on earth to do. Imagine, remembering so early in life! She stands at the threshold of a four day and night fast in the mountain wilderness and declares, with those innocent gypsy eyes, that she is a death midwife.

Her father was a little crazy. He called her a whore and treated her like dirt. Her mother's next husband tried to seduce his stepdaughter. It was not an easy childhood. Adolescence was filled with disappointments. And all the while she knew that she would usher people through the gates of death.

Two days ago I talked with her. She told me she would be glad to be of assistance to me on the day I died. I can't pretend to understand a woman like this. I can only admire, respect, and, with memories of death hungering for my soul, desire to possess the idea of her, to identify her as a special angel of the death goddess.

Actually, when I think of her I find myself resisting death. It is too sweet, too fitting, too right, too real to trust an angel of death. I retreat to my everyday life. I try not to think about that young woman. I even tell myself she's a figment of my imagination.

But I know she's there, in the pumping of my heart, in the rage of breath, watching me. She's smiling, and, like any dear friend, hoping I won't need her. But someday, I will.

About the time I met M, I had been toying with the idea that I was an unknowing player in some ingenious drama to initiate me into true manhood. The idea certainly isn't new to novelists and screen writers. Along the way, she would facilitate a series of experiences and events that would deepen my soul and my ability to love.

Twenty-six years later, I see that this initiatory way of looking at life wasn't so absurd. If you feel "called," you have to take this point of view. I rummage through my memory banks for those special "growth events." I was as raw a candidate as ever stepped across the threshold. There were times when M virtually stood on her head to get me to understand something, or to actually see her. And then there were all those people who came to study with us, many of whom (I swear!) were part of the conspiracy. Some of the most effective initiatory experiences had to do with guilt and redemption, ego and ego-death, profanity and sacredness. The passage to the boudoir of Anima was frightening and arduous.

Looking back on it, I can see how I was tested.

I always came back for more. Why? I am quite sure I am no different than you.

I know others who have had to be far more tenacious than me. I am a private in their army. But we all share in this one thing. We remembered that we had been "called."

I love the tales of those old prophets lusting after the silence and loneliness of the desert. Something out there in the distances pulled them toward the center of nowhere. They went like puppies to the tit. The nights were freezing; the days were searing hot. The stones lacerated their feet. Their mouths cracked and bled. They saw shards of God in burning bushes, angels, flocks of ravens, painted horses. They thought they heard small voices in the blackness.

The desert swallowed them up. Sometimes they were never heard from again. Sometimes their bones were found rotting in a lion's den.

Were they trying to remember the way to God?

The desert is God calling to those who are willing to obey the terms of every human "find me dance"—and behind each veil of God lurks another veil, a deeper Goddess.

What is the use in obeying the call when you never quite see the God Without Clothes? Who cares? Does Goddess care? My memory tells me that the desert is as close to death as I will ever get in life.

I love the desert.

It's the last veil between me and the day I will lie under a Creosote bush in dead summer and wish so anxiously for water that it will come, impossibly flowing like a river from a high glacier.

❖❖❖

Once an event becomes memory, it must be lived with. But the psyche is often reluctant to commit certain events to memory, accustomed to pain or guilt. The "avoidance factor." We tell ourselves that if we do not avoid what we remember as painful, sooner or later we will self-destruct. We say no, and turn away, fearing all too well the consequences.

So, what about those who do self-destruct? Those who repeatedly find pleasure in experiences their memories tell them will be painful? What's going on with these people? Don't they know better?

Here we have to take a step up, to avoid psychological theorizing, and answer this question from the perspective of "the calling."

The call comes from We Who Have Gone Before. One way or another, we struggle to obey the call, to live out its terms. If we are called to live the life of a saint, or at least a relatively good person, we find ourselves challenged to do so. If we are called to be an alcoholic or a masochist, we somehow find a challenge (and an inverted pleasure) in doing so.

Is there any way we can alter the call, thwart its outworkings in our genes and ways? Yes, we can live other lives, and commit ourselves to other callings, but the old calling, the one served up by the sacred ancestors, runs deep. They say, "once a junky always a junky."

But not quite. We Who Have Gone Before have another name too. Free Will.

She told me to remember to stop at the store on the way home. I made a mental note to remind myself. Then I drove out to the Eureka Valley. I wrote a note to myself and put it on the seat of the car. Then I took a walk. When I came back to the car, the note lay on the seat. It said, "Store."

Thinking, as I left the desert, that I still might forget, I put the note into a pocket next to my heart. As I drove home I told myself, "Don't forget to stop at the store."

Then something a woman had said to me the day before floated into my mind. The remark had hurt, and I was still trying to figure out what she had meant by it. Could she have been innocent of any guile?

Maybe I was putting too much importance on the whole conversation. As I pulled into the driveway, I realized I was going to have to ask the woman to clarify her remark. I walked into the house. My wife greeted me in the kitchen. "Did you stop at the store?"

I'm dismayed at how easily I forget. Short-term, long-term—it doesn't matter. It could be worse, no doubt. But it's bad enough. And I wonder how many others are afflicted with the same malady.

Why do we forget? If we are, in fact, children of memory, if we give birth to memory, if the Great Mother remembers us, then why should we forget?

Perhaps there is a need to forget, something inside us that craves the poignancy of forgetting, that cannot be lured away from blanking out, that wants to drop the burden of remembering.

Can it be that the psyche, the same psyche that governs the workings of nature, craves to exist without a past? This makes sense. But there is an equal craving for the future, so that tomorrow can be remembered.

The twin streams of remembering and forgetting dance together in the cosmic masquerade called the present. Tomorrow is born from the need to remember what has been forgotten.

Remembering is an act of re-creation. The past is born anew, an altered version of an event in time. This re-creation occurs in relational opposition to the forces of de-creation, the forces of forgetting. It's like the ancient struggle between darkness and light.

Thus it is perfectly reasonable to assume that we—like all of our brothers and sisters on this planet—have been remembered, re-created by the universe, in order to be forgotten—so that we can again be remembered.

Selene Foster: Photo transfer and mixed media on rice paper, '99

Fall has arrived and the bufflehead ducks have come back to our lake. On their way south, they need the food our shoreline can give them. Year by year they remember to drop in. They're regular as clockwork. Other birds too. M said she saw a flock of vultures heading south along the foothills of the mountains. Going down to Mexico.

Can you imagine a flock of vultures hunched together in a tree like a bunch of wise guys, not saying a word to each other, when suddenly, as one, they arise from the branches? Time to go!

Group telepathy. Maybe humans have this gift too. Yesterday the vultures of Big Pine seemed to be satisfied with the leavings beside Highway 395. It was a nice day. No sign of the winter to come.

Actually, there was a difference in the air, an infinitesimal chill that only vultures could feel. Brrr. Time to go.

Humans have also been so blessed.

Speaking of memory! Not only the day, the hour, the second, but the route and the destination. Every year a remembering, a re-creation of the ancient, ancestral past. Every year, an enactment defying extinction.

The migration reaffirms the power of the dark forces of forgetting—by summoning the equally powerful forces of remembering.

"Forget." Literally, "to go without getting." The word comes from the Old German: "to miss or lose one's hold." To slip, to stumble, to trip, to lose balance or control.

When I was slicing tomatoes I fore-got. I lost my hold on the knife because I lost my grip on what I was doing. I'll have to go back and pick up my finger and do it right this time.

When I look at my life this way I see how often I fore-get. I tell myself that forgetting has a lot to do with learning and growing. By losing our grip just before we get it, we learn how to hold on. "Going without getting," we re-member.

Many years ago I got lost in the thick forests of the Cascade Range in Washington. I was hiking alone along a logging road, struck off cross-country for a lake, and never found the trail again. I couldn't have been lost for more than 5 hours—but it seemed an eternity. Darkness was coming on. In my panic, I crashed through the underbrush and nearly broke my leg. When I came to myself, I remembered. The ravine into which I had worked myself actually led down to the place where I'd parked my car.

What has always fascinated me is the question: Why did I forget? Why did I deliberately allow myself to become disoriented? I think it was because, as I was hiking along, I was "going without getting." My psyche was restlessly, randomly seeking to anchor itself in the personal events of those days—which included the breakdown of my marriage. I was stumbling without being aware. I was out of control. I was fore-getting.

Memory is easily distracted. It opens door after door, frantic for the light. And it is positively compulsive in its craving for images, fantasies, daydreams, that tug the psyche away from everyday concerns. But when the chips are down, when we hit the skids, when we go lower than low, memory stops looking for the light. It lies down with us in a fetal position and cheers the dawning of a long labor. Faithfully, it feeds our psyche with all the dark, unhappy memories it can muster, stuffing gloom and more gloom into the maw of depression.

Why does memory do this to us? Why does it have to lead us into the dark? Can it be that, in terms of memory's ultimate goal of survival—we have to find our way through the seemingly impossible?

The night sky is spangled with stars.

SECRETS AND ROMANCE

Is there anyone who does not keep a secret or two locked up in a box in a back drawer of the psyche? No doubt there are those who claim to be an "open book." Such folks tend to be boring—and dangerous. They think they are being open-minded when actually they are being devious, and cannot admit to themselves that they are hiding all kinds of prejudices and ulterior motives, mostly self aggrandizing.

Give me the honest ones who concede to having a few secrets. Give me the mysterious ones who wrestle with memory monsters in the privacy of their own beds. Give me the souls who labor up the hill with secrets big as Sisyphus' boulder. Verily, they are learning, step by step, the motivating power of secrecy.

Secrets can be used for good or bad. For example, a shameful or guilty secret, like an inner billboard, can motivate a person to do much good in the world—or much evil. The saint and the rapist are both plagued by memories of sex. The saint uses his memories of sex to love and care for others. The rapist uses his memories of sex to injure others.

Secrets are potent medicine. Consider the power of a secret love to disrupt a life, to cause sleeplessness, distract eating patterns, motivate the other party to pine away. Consider the power of a secret crime to gnaw at sanity, to consume both victim and victimizer with guilt and self-abhorrence.

We must never underestimate the power of a secret to manifest itself in the physical world, for good or ill.

Memories that are locked up in special boxes and opened only at certain times have a way of coming out of their hiding places and demanding to be attended to. Secrecy and compulsion to tell are related.

That which is hidden seeks to become manifest. This urge of the closed toward openness, the imprisoned toward freedom, the inarticulate toward expression. . . . One of the most important elements in what we humans call character.

Let's go back to the beginning. According to the story, God kept a certain secret from Adam and Eve. He said, "See that luscious tree over there? It's a no no." He didn't tell them why. The secret He was keeping from them was, in fact, the secret of mortality. If they got into the cookie jar they would have to leave Paradise and live by the sweat of their brow, and labor to give birth to children, and die. Did He want his children to know that?

The secrets of mortality are too alluring to be denied. We are all naked and in cahoots with Lucifer. The more we hide the truth from ourselves, the more the secret prevails. The offspring of Adam and Eve were Cain and Abel. . . .

Cain was a meat-eater. Abel was a vegetarian. One generation into the revelation of the secret and we have a proper diet murder on our hands?

You can see why God tried to keep this mortality business secret. But not even immortality could shroud the truth. Sooner or later we wake up naked and remember who we are.

❖❖❖❖

Erotic secrets can be the most potent of all. Nursed inwardly for fear of ridicule, misunderstanding, or shame, they can mushroom like cancers and block the normal flow of time. Or they can become pleasure-fuel for the addict, who returns to them again and again through a locked safe with a familiar combination. Or they can become actual behavior, like fantasies made true to life, and suddenly we are on a roller coaster ride, scared but not sure we want to get off, and we know there might be grave consequences, and we just don't care.

I still have a few sexual secrets that I've never told to anyone. Sometimes, when I am all alone and fasting on the mountain, the hidden memory will rise to consciousness, and all at once the stones will look like breasts, the stumps like penises, the mouse holes like vaginas. My body begins to shiver. My stomach sinks and a knot forms in my groin. I feel like I need to take a shit, or do something about the feeling down there. The temptation to masturbate is strong. I want to fuck the trees, the wind, the cactus, anything.

Now these secrets that so perturb me are, in fact, memories—secret memories held inwardly, never told, and opened only when I am completely alone, when I am totally free to indulge myself. I can't imagine that I am alone in this. Nature's on my side. Other species of the wilderness aren't the least bit inhibited about doing it. They must be remembering sexy episodes all the time, like how it felt to dance and kiss and copulate. Their memories must saturate my universe with the stuff that swells my penis and makes me want to come.

The real secret is this: unlock the secret box in your heart and you will unlock the door between yourself and the erotic nature of We Who Have Gone Before.

Nature is filled with secrets: hiding places, camouflage, stealthy actions. Night hides, obscures, conceals. The entire physical substance of nature is nothing but a mask. What's behind all this concealment?

When you look behind, underneath, inside, on the other side, and then measure the hair rising on the back of your neck, you might see the naked truth. It could be the actual shape of the rabbit hiding in the brush. It could be a horned toad looking exactly like the sand. It could be the mountain lion peering at your campfire from the shadows of the trees. Don't go away. There is more. Behind the secret lies another secret. Behind the rabbit is the energy system called Rabbit. Behind the rabbit energy system is memory. One of these memories is Lion hunting Rabbit.

Memory is the rabbit remembering to be a rabbit. And beyond it all, beyond the secrets of flesh and bone and cell and protein and molecule and electron of rabbit, lies the ultimate secret of memory.

The sheer existence of nature is predicated on the essence of Rabbit remembering to be.

All this hiding and concealment and secretive behavior? All those rabbits who have gone before—remembering.

You go on a vision fast. You climb the sacred mountain and you lie like a secret in the secret of the night beneath the secret of the stars. Maybe it will occur to you that you are here in this secret place because the secret creator of the secret stars remembered to secret you here.

A bumblebee came nosing around today, looking for blooms. But flowers are few and far between. Four inches of rain fell this year in the northern Mojave. Everything but the cactus and the creosote seem to be struggling.

In drought years, pollination slows down. Still, romance happens. Certain species suffer loss, but survive somehow—barring unforeseen catastrophic changes. There won't be so many bumblebees and hummingbirds next year, but they *will* be. The only pollinator I saw all day was a yellow beavertail cactus blossom squirming with ants, beatles, flies, wasps. That one flower was insuring the continuation of insect, reptile, and bird life for miles around.

Among humans, one of the most cogent symbols of romance is pollination: "Something in the air" presages continuance. Among humans, romance apparently occurs regardless of the circumstances. It even blooms in times of war and natural catastrophe.

It may be that, like all the other species, humans are programmed to over-romance when times are hard. Note how much of commercial television is dedicated to pollination, covering up drought conditions by strewing flowers and syrupy music all over the screen.

People say times are good: "Just take a look at the stock market." I don't agree. We may have been persuaded by an inflated American lifestyle that there are flowers everywhere, and we're dead wrong. Hard times are here and they're not going to get better. Already, there are too many of us—even while other species are dying off. What makes us think we are doing just fine when we are murdering our neighbors? Or when our neighbors are out to murder us?

There aren't enough blossoms to go around.

Are we caught in a memory trance of childish (but innocent) love, sex, romance—thereby forgetting our place on the earth? Maybe so. But we are also unconsciously remembering what we as a species do when times are bad.

This ancient memory, graven in our genes, is not appropriate anymore. Consumption has created a drought, and into an ever increasing emptiness we keep romancing, like bacteria in an open wound. First rocks, then spears, then guns, then semi-automatic rifles, then biological terror, then thermonuclear bombs.

Make safe sex, not war.

I, the father of three children (and two abortions) write this—just another stupid idiot watching the sun set on the Funeral Mountains of Death Valley.

The wheezing, Swiss cheese-lunged man of 63 still wants to be romanced, lusted after, even though he can go no more than 15 minutes before he winds up prostrate and panic-stricken at the edge of the bed. Gripped by the fear that he will not get enough air to breathe, his penis goes soft and he suffers the most excruciating embarrassment. Why should his wife want to make love to him, when virile, handsome men laugh lustily in the training circle every day? After all, she is almost fifteen years younger than he, without a blemish or sign of ill health.

I tell you, romance blooms in strange places. I can't rightly say what generates it. There must be some memory in us that finds disfigurement, physical disease, even terminal illness attractive. And I wonder, is this true of all the species? Or is it some gift that Grandmother Nature has remembered to give to humans? Indeed, it seems to be something more than just sex and propagation of the species. M still gets excited when we make love. I assume she actually wants to be with the old cripple.

What's going on? Why should romance bloom in the most barren soil, when old age and death are nigh? What possible utilitarian good does it serve? Here is where I differ sharply from many biologists. They would call these feelings I describe nothing but "mating behavior." I would call them romance.

And I wonder why such "feelings" exist in the human species.

It is no secret that the greatest rite of passage is parenthood. Renee, I want to tell you that. Yes, I know you were on the verge of a brilliant career. We have rarely seen such an amazing mixture of beauty, intelligence, and creative energy in a young woman—tried by some of the darkest powers—yet ready to take them all on. How could anyone have known you without remarking about the promising way you were walking your path?

Life's biggest test has begun. From the moment your eyes glazed over with desire and you gave yourself to that handsome, radiant man, the romance bell rang above the initiation grounds. The twin boys that came forth were no secret to Mother Nature. She had dreamed of you and that young man and the twins from the beginning of time. We can hardly defy our Mother. What she remembers happens.

Some call this kind of memory Coyote. No doubt, Mother Earth would do the same if she were called Baboon. She has this habit of opening her legs to her lover, one of whom is called "We Who Have Gone Before." What comes forth from their union is a fledgling, a foundling. And if she did not possess what we humans call "maternal instincts," her children would die, or grow twisted, of no use to her kindred.

Who will provide for the growth and well-being of the young? The human answer to this dilemma is the rites of passage of parenthood. Has there ever been any other answer? No.

So these are the terms of the rites of passage of parenthood— that the mother and father give of their substance, their dreams, their spirit, their romantic selves, so that the passage can be completed. This is the supreme test of the winter shield. Selfless love for others. Only in this kind of love is the true nature of womanhood, or manhood, known.

Renee, I honor you for undertaking these rites of passage. In time, your restless imagination will tangle with much more than children. The world waits for you to inherit your destiny.

"Romance." The Oxford Dictionary of English Etymology is of no help. It defines the word "romance" as "a tale in verse embodying adventure, esp. of medieval legend. . . fictitious narrative in prose." And it traces the word to "the vernacular tongue (as distinct from literary Latin), i.e., work composed from this."

I can go with this definition only in the sense that romance is from the language of the people, from the vernacular tongue. It is not highfalutin' academic terminology. It is the slang of humanity, and it was born from thousands of years of remembering the experience of growth into maturity.

I saw romance in my own children, in their appetite for celluloid blood and thunder, love and peril, heroism and triumph. Death does not really exist for these childhood heroes and heroines, no matter how often they teeter at the brink of disaster. The guys they love and the women they adore are destined to be possessed forever—no matter how poignantly they are separated by circumstances of plot.

You may wonder what this has to do with reality. For me, every one of these romances holds a tiny, overwhelmingly important shred of reality. Like puzzle pieces, I can fit them all together into the rites of passage I invented for myself to reach manhood. In a very real sense, they were reality, as translated by the mythic urges of imagination.

I'm simply not willing to file "romance" under "frivolous." The sacred ancestors gave me to understand that there were sacred worlds into which I could venture, where the ordinary laws of reality did not apply. In these worlds there was great peril, and great reward. And, in the end, everything would come out all right. A magical leap would have been made. I would be richer, fuller, wiser, and more complete. I would have become a little more of a man.

Even as I open the Book of Death, I'm still reading in the vernacular, in the mass unconsciousness of the "common people." I can't stop believing in the fairy tale.

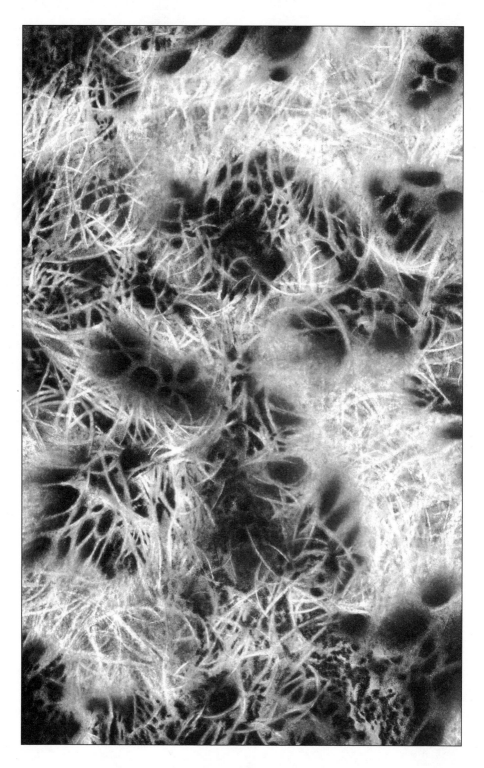

Selene Foster: Photo transfer and mixed media on rice paper, '99

DEPRESSION AND TERROR

They even knew about it in my childhood Baptist church. The elders called it the "mountain top experience." You went off to church summer camp for a week or two, or you went forward to the altar to "accept Jesus as your savior." You got high, real high. But then you had to come down from your mountain. You had to face reality. Your faith had to be tested. That's when the going got rough—when you had to live in the world of unbelief, when, as John Bunyan put it, you stumbled into the "slough of despond."

It's not easy to come down. I recall a time when I was a hippie, when I simply didn't want to come down. If I started to backslide, I dropped another hit. Secretly, I knew that I would have to come down sooner or later. Finally, I got so strung out I had to descend. When I did, I hit bottom.

Memory is a fickle thing. One day we are as high as a kite and deeply, unabashedly in love with ourselves. The next day the plumbing won't work and we have fallen out of love with our life. We don't seem to be very good at living on the laurels of the past. Don't ask me why. Ask memory. Why can't we simply reach back and relive a moment of personal ecstasy, and so flood the present gloom with light? We can, but usually it takes time and patience to bait the hook, throw out the line, and land a BIG ONE.

I tell myself the reason why I keep reeling in an empty hook is so that I can keep throwing out the bait again.

The man who wrote the manuscript I am currently reading is a believer in Higher Consciousness and Spiritual Mastery. He doesn't hold emotions in very high esteem. I differ with him on this point. Emotions are as sacred as enlightenment. Emotions are a path to enlightenment.

But I hear him say, "Emotions lead to feelings of depression. Depression is not our true state. We should not have to go there. If we were unattached, we would not have to go there. . ." and so on. Sure, if you see life that way, go for it.

In the meantime, I'll hang with the passionate, the transparent, the mortal ones who are tossed to and fro on the seas of emotion. I may not be above it all, but at least I'm burning.

No doubt, some of us get carried away. Overcome by passion, we lose control, brutalize, rape, kill, make war, commit suicide. Passion can carry us anywhere. It can carry us to hell. It can carry us to enlightenment. And if we ride on the bucking back of passion, we can expect to get to enlightenment via the road to hell.

I hear this way is called "The Road of Com [with] passion."

The treasure lies down there, hidden, like a pocket of crystals deep inside a granite boulder. We get to the treasure by heading in the opposite direction. We go down, down, into the despair of ever finding the treasure. We descend into the darkness of ourselves, where there seems to be no hope, no escape, no light. Memories of incapacity and victimization, livid with self-disgust, worm their way into our souls and erupt into open sores. Our feelings howl like wounded dogs. We wonder if we have any reason to go on living.

Just about the time we reach the end of the line in a cave winding deeper, ever deeper, into the Mountain of Resignation, we stumble across the treasure. It is ours for the taking—but we hardly notice it is there, preoccupied as we are with our pain.

Still, we picked up a half-buried crystal and idly turned it over in our hands. We could just as well have been holding a lump of coal. Writhing like any wretch beneath the thumb of hopelessness, we cannot help but paint everything, even the crystal, black.

No matter. The treasure continues to lie there in the gloom, waiting to be seen for what it is. Sooner or later, the glint will catch our eyes. Suddenly we will realize how bored we are with distraction. We will look more intently at the treasure in the palm of our hand. We pick it up again, inspect it more closely. Ah! A lump of coal! If I light it, it will keep me warm.

When I was a young man, in a fit of despair I took a steel rod out of the gate and beat myself over the head until senseless. When I came to myself, I was lying wet, cold and naked in the early-morning dew. I went into a depression that lasted for a year.

Such a growth-event pales in comparison to many. I am fortunate to have been spared the worst. After all, my depression was self-precipitated. A man from Rwanda whose wife was raped and murdered before his very eyes, wants to come to our school. A woman student tells the story of having been raped at knife point by a gang of adolescent boys. Another man speaks of the death of his wife in an automobile accident from which he emerged, unscathed. There is no end to stories of, or reasons for, the deepest kinds of despair. Dear god, how deep can deep get?

So an event unfolded before our horrified eyes and we were powerless to stop it. Quite possibly we were making it happen to ourselves. Years later, we remembered the event unexpectedly and we were plunged into a living hell. All at once we were crushed by memory-feelings so powerful and vivid we couldn't even tread water. The current pulled us down into the regions of never never and we began to drown.

What did we do?

We found a thread, a gleam, a gem, the tiniest corner of a window down there in the straight jacket room. How did we find it? Not by looking for it. We found it by being blind. We found it by feeling so sorry for ourselves and so victimized that we thought we had nowhere else to go but suicide.

But we didn't self-destruct. We decided to live. We saw how we were going to live. The details might not have been very clear, but all at once the lungs were crying for breath and there was something we had to do. Maybe all we did was to get up from our bed of pain, turn on the light, go into the bathroom, and wash our face. There was a course of action, a way. Suddenly we allowed there to be one positive memory of ourselves, one fondest dream—something we knew, deep down inside, that was uniquely us.

That little memory let in just enough light to see by. Just enough to remind us that we did not want to be living in the dungeon of self-indulgence.

Clutching that priceless memory, we groped our way out of the cave. When we emerged, the blindness faded from our eyes and we saw that everything had changed.

No, we had changed.

Our friend Gigi belongs to the "Dark Institute." She goes around recruiting people to attend courses. You don't have to do much to qualify for admission. All you have to do is to acknowledge that you get depressed—and that you are a student of your depression. Almost everyone she meets wants to belong to the "Institute." I like the idea of studying at the School of Depression. But it's so "uncool" these days. If you have been enlightened by the gurus of the New Age, you drop the ugly like a hot potato. You don't lay darkness on yourself, or on other people. You radiate light. You go about shedding love-pollen on everyone.

A group of Africans from Rwanda declared their interest in coming to our School. In 1994, a million people were killed in their homeland, when the Hutus set out to massacre their rival Tutsis. 100,000 children were orphaned. One out of every two citizens of Rwanda saw a loved one killed. And this particular horror is but one of many. Consider Afghanistan. Consider Israel-Palestine. Consider Bosnia. Consider the USA.

Gigi is absolutely right. There is a good reason for the Dark Institute to exist, and to accept enrollees any time of the year, at any age, race, gender, or station. Yes, it's true that the only way we could think of to really turn people around so that they could see a reason for the Dark Institute to be, was to put them in the wilderness for four days and nights without food or company or shelter. No doubt there are other ways. But this one struck to the core. It had to be. People had to get in touch with their own dark memories before they could fully engage the memories of others who dwelled in darkness.

I say hooray! Let's get down in the dirt and look at our own shit. Let's see how we're connected to everybody else's shit. Let's not pretend that we have found some new way to keep our toes clean. As old Rabbi Buber said, Rake the dirt this way. Rake the dirt that way. It's still dirt.

People ask me, how do I get out of this depression? I always say, Go out and be alone on the earth and remember who and where you are. Yes, they say, but what if that just makes me more depressed?

Well, there is depression and there is the Great Depression. Depression is temporary. The Great Depression runs deeper and is caused by the Human Condition. Normal depression is caused by many things—environment, social conditions, personal loss, frustration, guilt, trauma, hormonal and chemical imbalances, etc. The Great Depression is caused by the soul's unhappiness with the prospect of death, an eventuality that cannot be remedied.

If it just makes you more depressed with a small "d," then get on with the challenge of Big D. Unless you're a basket case, and you're not, you'll find your way along like all the rest of us. If you have fallen into the Great Depression, then you are discovering what the rest of humanity all too often ignores. Brushing up close to death can be the most awesome experience humans suffer. Even if it is a chemical imbalance that is causing the trouble, congratulations! You have eyeballed the jaws of the real monster.

One of the most powerful expressions of the soul's discontent with death is Psyche's swoon, as described by the Roman story teller, Apuleius. Captivated by a kiss stolen from the god of love, Psyche seeks him in every hiding place, including those in herself. Finally, she arrives at the gates of the immortal palace of Eros, as if dead, and can only be revived by a return-kiss from the God himself. The happy ending does not dispel the truth: Death is a long, dark swoon. And Love is the only thing that can save us eternally.

The most powerful teaching of the Great Depression is that We Who Have Gone Before are in love with Eros.

Therefore, we stand a chance of immortality.

Elohim was wrong. His children were never able to completely eliminate Ishmael and the outcast of Israel. Terror begat terror, for four thousand years until now. If you murder me or my children, my grandchildren and great grandchildren remember. If I murder you, your grandchildren and great grandchildren remember.

We can't kill memory. Who do we think we are? If God couldn't do it, then who are we to wage war against We Who Have Gone Before?

The deepest memory of our sacred ancestors tells us that war begets war, that terrorism begets terrorism, and that no matter what happens, the people always suffer and remember, especially the children. We know this unequivocally. Even the most brutal and unthinking male, regardless of country or nationality, knows this. Even Hitler, Edi Amin, Pol Pot, Gengis Khan, the Africaaners, Stalin, Cortez, Nero, Nixon, Osama Bin Laden, knew this, deep inside their feverish psyches. But they were mere children who had never grown into full maturity as human beings. They reacted with the instinctive fear-logic of children. If it's scary, make it go away. They were of no use to the human race—except as examples of what we must avoid.

Revenge does not make a man or a woman of a child. Revenge only creates more ghosts and feelings of loss and desolation. When will we learn? Can we not open our ears to what those who have gone before are saying to us? "Go the other way!" they scream. "Don't make the same mistakes! Proceed toward our collective evolutionary destiny!" Even though we are in the midst of overwhelming pain and grief, there must be another way, if only for the sake of the children.

Suicide bombing. Self-obliteration because you hate someone else so much you are ready to kill yourself in order to be rewarded with Paradise. Not what you would call ordinary suicide. Nevertheless, this kind of blind faith has existed from the beginning of human time, and is true of all mythological systems. How many of us would sacrifice our lives by killing as many of the "enemy" as possible in order to save or revenge our own families, loved ones, or precious beliefs?

It's an old, old memory, this suicide-terror stuff. You can't just snuff it out in 500,000 years. One of the habit-memories inherited by humans is a psychological condition called "self-righteousness" or "we-righteousness." Because our values are inherently right, my values are inherently right. War itself is nothing more than a form of suicide-terrorism. I will put my body on the bloody line because you must be snuffed out.

Of course it doesn't quite work that way. There are no victors. There are only memories.

Selene Foster: Mixed media on paper, '99

Even though we would rather not have to think about it, hoping desperately to find a pleasant life without the threat of death, we awake to new dawns of terror and fear. We have not yet made the distinction between faith and truth.

Try to murder memory. Go ahead. Kill it. It doesn't matter which country, faith, culture we belong to. With the same overwhelming violence and cunning, wipe out what happened to our loved ones. Wipe out those who are responsible for their deaths. Wipe out our own pain and grief by giving ourselves to revenge.

Not even vengeance will wash our sufferings away. The memory will remain.

I wonder about all the other animals. Are they motivated by such emotions as revenge? Does the tree avenge itself on the forest fire? Does the worm avenge itself on the plow? Does the woodpecker avenge the loss of its eggs to the magpie? Does the chipmunk take revenge on the hawk? Does the dolphin retaliate against the drag net?

Yet there are examples of nature taking revenge. The dog who finally turns on an abusive owner. The whale that rams the harpooner. The lion that turns rogue. The cockroach that returns in greater numbers. The weeds that grow from poisoned soil. Mother Nature has been known to seek retaliation, in her own way and time, by returning the poison to the land on which her creatures feed. She returns radiation to the rivers, plagues and death to her own kind. Sometimes, where she has been hurt, she fights back with new growth, inimical to her offspring who live upon that land.

Is terrorism Nature's way of taking revenge on humans? Has she built revenge into the human psyche? Humans in particular seem prey to this memory. Is this her way of striking back at the poisons we spread and the violence we wreak? The war against terrorism. Terrorism's war against terrorism. Back and forth, death against death—until the people are weary of the shedding of blood, and both sides call a truce—for a little while.

Is Nature capable of premeditated terrorism? Does she think about it or does she simply do it? Is Nature conscious, like human beings? Did she not give birth to human beings? How else can she control populations? Nature seeks balance, and her human creatures have thrown her into turmoil. No doubt she will find a means to get back into balance.

The time has come to be terrified—not of our brother and sister humans—but of our Nature.

Life is cheap. Life is dear. Life is nothing and everything. Death is cheap. Death is dear. Death is nothing and everything. The tiny bean sprout, braving its way into the sun and rain. Is it not cheap? Is it not dear? Is it not nothing and everything? The raving terrorist, arising from the underground to murder in order to be heard. Is he not cheap? Is he not dear? Is he not nothing and everything? You who speak for God. Are you not cheap? Are you not dear? You who speak for the devil. Are you not cheap? Are you not dear? Are not good and evil nothing and everything? Who speaks for the truth of nothing and everything? Does a single human life speak for truth? Does a fresh water snail? Does the German Brown trout who gobbles the snail? Does the bait on a hook at the end of a line held by a human to catch a German Brown speak for the truth of nothing and everything?

Evil and good. Here we go again. Good must win out over evil. But the question remains. Who has the right to speak for good? Who has the right to speak for evil? Are we not nothing and everything?

One of those big troop helicopters just went over the house, probably heading down to the Naval Base at China Lake from the Marine base at Sonora Pass. I thought about all the young soldiers riding in it. They might indeed be on the front line of another war against terrorism, some of them still longing for the taste of mother's milk. Hate grows like yeast within the human psyche, and easily becomes the primary reason to wage war, to wipe the human face off those suspected, so that innocent life can be taken.

So many perish behind the charismatic leadership of a few. Public outrage is manipulated by those who seek to be re-elected or appreciated. No doubt many of our leaders have a "feminine side," a soft side, a love for their wives and children, a hope for future peace. But their knees jerk and they forget that hate crimes against humanity breed hate crimes against humanity.

Long ago, the wages of hate became clear to We Who Have Gone Before. Why else would the collective dream of peace be with us still?

You kill my mother? I kill your daughter. And so the war against terror rages on, and the perpetrators keep escaping, like rats into holes behind the refrigerator or the toilet. And the innocent people who are simply trying to survive in a terrible time? They are sacrificed in the war to kill the rats.

Rats appear to be quite adapted to human civilization, perhaps even more so than we. They may live long after humans are gone.

So what are we to do with terrorists? What are we to do with rats? Can we eradicate them? Impossible. Do we let them rummage under the covers while we are sleeping? Absolutely not. Do we poison them with godawful substances that get into the bloodstreams of our cat, our dog, our food, and the rest of our karmic life? They will survive by the skin of their sharp tiny teeth and come back in greater numbers. Or do we contain them, as best we can, and try to create a world in which rats and humans can somehow peacefully, though painfully, co-survive?

The question is basic to human civilization: What do we do with our brothers and sisters who are too far gone to rescue? Do we ignore them, do we contain them, do we capture them, do we kill them? If we kill them, they will return again.

Okay, so "the powers that be" call in the Exterminators, and the Ratbusters come in with all kinds of fancy gear, and when it is over we pay them a good sum of money to tell us the problem is solved.

A few months later, the rats are back in the Wheaties again. They ate the poison laid out for them, and some of them died horribly, but a few wastrels survived, found a little bit of sex together, and now their children raven with hunger.

At least the Exterminators have fatter wallets.

Forgiveness, Fermentation, Nostalgia, and Violence

What is this thing we humans call "forgiveness?" Isn't it a strange idea? That we should forgive those who hurt us? Is it—or is it not—perfectly natural to forgive?

One of William Blake's *Proverbs of Hell* says: "The cut worm forgives the plow." What could that crazy old mystic have meant by that? Was he implying that the lowly worm is conscious enough to entertain altruistic impulses? That the lowly worm, in the throes of decapitation, is capable of such a sophisticated understanding of its own fate as to forgive the impersonal scythe?

Surely, worms do not have feelings. What a fatuous notion, to ascribe human emotions to nonhuman species. How can we say they feel as we do? Or if they feel at all?

Then why should I care what the worm is feeling? Why should I want to live down there in the moist dirt and experience the knife severing me from life? Why should I want to know anything about the psychology of the lowly worm? Am I some kind of freak?

As I cling to my purchase on the sacred mountain of life's dream, I feel the darkness coming, the stars winking on. I find myself caring about the feelings of the worm—and about all the creatures, great and small, who share this tiny grain of earth with me. When the time comes, they will be very happy when I am served to them on a silver platter.

It is time to stand on my own two feet and declare myself. I am a human being and a poet. And I care about how the worm feels. And I do wonder, with a strange, deathward yearning, if the worm—and all other creatures on this improbable earth—are as capable (or as incapable) of forgiveness as humans.

Is forgiveness a plot written into our morphogenetic nature?

Is it not a curious notion, that we should need to ask God for forgiveness? Does the twisted juniper in the high mountains need to ask forgiveness for growing twisted? Does the wild burro who fouls the springs in the desert mountains need to ask God for forgiveness? Does the gopher ravaging the potatoes in my garden? Does the wild goose sucked into the intake of a 707 (causing it to crash and take the lives of hundreds of humans) need to ask for forgiveness? Does the man, lured into "sin" by the "forces of darkness," need to ask God for forgiveness?

Could it be that the tragic and religious distinction between "good" and "evil," so evident in the Christianity, has been the cause of untold plots of forgiveness and revenge? I cannot keep from asking why God, who created us, who said He would love us unconditionally (*if* we asked Him for forgiveness and lived for *Him*)—would be so revengeful.

"You can believe my promise that you shall have eternity," He said. And what if we don't "believe" Him? Then we can go to Hell?

That we should be so entangled with a childhood conception of the Almighty is an old story—but not the oldest. The oldest, and the most long-lived, tells a different story. It says we act like all the other creatures on this earth, that we are all the other creatures on this earth, that we must ask for forgiveness of each other because we must depend on each other, and respect each other, and look out for each other.

Take your pick. Look at the rainbow path unwinding ahead, your pilgrim's road of light and dark. Which memories truly serve you? Which will serve you best when you die?

Forgiveness is the best kind of therapy. A woman called to "dump" on me. Something I had said to her 15 years ago. It had just been an offhand remark, hardly conscious, and I had forgotten it. Suddenly I was standing in the judgment hall, and the witness for the prosecution was listing every grievance anybody had ever had with me. I winced and became quite inarticulate. In the deepest core of my being, I felt convicted.

But then, the accusations and the weeping ended. "Thank you for listening," she said, calmly. "I just want you to know I love you. I just want you to know I forgive you."

When she forgave me, peace swept through me like a river of oxygen. I realized the rest of my life would be bearable. I remembered that I was, after all, a reasonably decent person.

Selene Foster: Acrylic, ink, and charcoal on paper, '01

I thanked her for forgiving me. And then she thanked me for forgiving her.

How life can confound us! Years ago, at the very time I was beginning to smell the heady scent of my own destiny, my former wife of ten years fell in love with another. My universe shrank to a tiny passageway, seemingly too narrow for pain to work its way through. Nothing else mattered. I didn't give a hoot about the fact that the same thing had happened a billion times in the history of humankind. The despair was absolute and immediate. I went down to Hell.

I consider my reaction to be common, given the parameters of love. On one end we have those who will murder because they have been betrayed. On the other end we have those who will jump into bed and make it a threesome. In between we have all the different kinds of jealousies, and all the ways they are expressed.

Many years later, I was able to forgive my woman for this painful episode. And she forgave me for my reaction. When we both felt fully absolved, we were at peace with each other. We didn't feel embarrassed to be in each other's presence. We were healed.

When we were healed, we remembered all those centuries of betrayal and forgiveness!

Nostalgia: From the Greek *nostos* (return home) and *algos* (pain). Home sickness. Cloying memories of the past, the "glory days" of youth. Remembering with a chocked-up feeling of wishing it could be so again— the same feeling that beset and often becalmed the wide-ranging Odysseus on his journey to Ithaka. Home-pain. Longing for rest.

We watch this happen when our people return from the mountain of fasting and solitude. What seemed almost intolerable—their ordeal in the wilderness—often appears more preferable than returning to the body of the social world and all its demands. This reluctance usually involves the subject of "vision." Intent has been confirmed. The questers must live their new life station among the people. Their mountaintop perspective must be tested in the world-at-large.

That's when nostalgia rears its ugly head. They remember how damned good it was to be alone, without food and shelter, in the silence and beautiful reality of nature. And the more they remember, the more they wish they could go back there—crawling on their knees, if necessary—to that quiet, perfect niche among the rocks and trees, in the fresh, breeze-swept purchase of their power place.

The wilderness is our true home. It takes only a few days out there to realize it. We have come home. We belong here, in the home of our sacred ancestors, our legacy, our birthright.

Four days pass, ever so slowly, ever so quickly, and then we return from the mountain, to our home away from home, to our "temporary residence."

For the rest of our life we will try to get back to the sacred mountain. We will journey into the farthest reaches of boredom, routine, and conflict—and each passing moment, week, year, decade, will test our resolve to realize the vision, the way, the work, the path, that will finally bring us truly home.

We must not allow ourselves to be seduced by nostalgia. There is work to be done—engagement with the monsters and dragons of daily life, the siren calls, the seas of forgetfulness, the lures of foolishness and false bravado, the underworlds of karmic ghosts, the spells of sexuality, and the dark, passionate urge-dreams of sorcerers and sorceresses. There is no other way to get home.

We all journey with nostalgia. Sooner or later we come upon him standing beside the road, thumb out. He's such an old friend. We are compelled to stop and pick him up. How far you going, friend? Oh, up the road a piece. And so, for a while, nostalgia rides shotgun, and we go back in time and remember how it was, or how it might have been.

I have always considered nostalgia to be one of my darker visitors. I'm often dissatisfied with the present, feeling lonely, separate and unfulfilled. I think, if I could just change my reality and go back to the good old days. I chafe at events. I cannot resist thinking, "Ah, those were the good old days."

There was a time in my life when love came easy—or so says my memory—especially when I am being required by the terms of my life to work harder at loving.

So effortlessly nostalgia takes me back to the forever gone, and therefore oh so succulent days! Ah yes, I loved and was loved in a thousand pleasant ways. I was free then, free to express words and feelings that nowadays seem to choke in my throat. What has happened to me? Have I lost the beauty and the richness of days gone by? Am I doomed to wander the lonely road of a hard destiny?

Yet I know that most of these past events that enchant me so were not actually experienced as "enchanting." Memory seems to have glazed them over with whipped cream and cherries. Why should memory do things like that? Why should memory falsify the real event, make a mountain from a molehill, a silk purse from a sow's ear? Why should memories of the past beguile us away from the present?

From the cradle to the grave, life is filled with innocent pleasure. And memories respond to pleasure like iron filings to a magnet. But pleasure is fleeting. It ebbs and flows from the shores of the present like tidal effluvia. And it comes so mixed with other flotsam and jetsam that only rarely do we experience it as pure pleasure. How fortunate, then, that memory brings an event back into retrospect, different from the way it was first experienced—bigger, wider, and deeper.

I remember the first time my father took me fishing. My little brother tagged along and I was more than a little jealous that he should be included in something I wanted to happen exclusively between Dad and me. It was a beautiful day. The sun was shining on the creek. But the whole time I was at odds with my environment. The mosquitos were biting; the worm wouldn't conform to my hook; the line got tangled in the brush. Jumping from rock to rock, I stepped—tumbled—into the cold water. The last straw was when little brother caught the first fish while I was still trying to untangle my line from the currant bush.

Was I actually having as much fun as my memory tells me I was having that day?

When I soar back on the wings of nostalgia, I see the creek smoking with light. I see the sinuous forms of trout deep in the shadows. I see my father's hands, stained with soil and toil, showing me how to thread the worm on the hook. I hear his teaching voice, warm and steady. "Let the worm float into the current. That's it. Hold it. There's a big trout down there. I can see it."

I was having fun that day. I just didn't realize it then.

Sometimes, when I am fasting in the wilderness, I get very lonely for my civilized home. I wonder what am I doing here. This is especially true if I am pinned down by cold weather. I remember one fast at Death Valley Buttes when the rain turned to slush and for three days and nights the wind blew like a fury. For hours at a time I obsessed on home and a warm, dry bed. I couldn't see any reason for doing what I was doing and would have returned to the car if it had not seemed more uncomfortable to do so. I was glad when M came to my place, pleading in her eyes, and said, "Let's go home."

They say home is where the heart is. In that dark storm, my heart yearned for my "temporary home," for softness and warmth, and for more time in this all-too-short life to enjoy it.

Since then, I have always felt empathy with those who returned early from their fast. I know the power of homesickness. I even fear it. I don't want to become so attached to home that I cannot go someday to the home this life has been preparing for me. I cannot see exactly what this place will look like. I imagine it will be much like my own home, but I must not fail to include the storms that sweep in on the broom of time, when the ice forms on the window panes and the freezing wind moans under the eaves.

Memory underscores the power of home. There is, no doubt, a reason to harbor such strong and positive memories of our own place in this life. Like migrating birds, we go there when this life is complete—we go to the homes we have prepared for ourselves.

Even now, as I write about homesickness, I look around at the walls of my study. Cluttered, comfortable, and thoroughly mine. Not a bad place to go when I die.

There is something in us that will not wait. We want it all now. *Ahorita! Inmediamente!*

If the subject is transformation, then let's do it *now!* It's so intolerable here. Let's get on with it. Just tell me what I have to do.

Many come to Lost Borders with this item on their agendas. They have been enculturated by the "on demand" values of the material world from childhood, and know nothing else. If we need something, we can go down to the corner store; we can order it over the internet; we can take a pill.

For many of those who come to Lost Borders, "transformation" is the magic bait. They think, well, if I just go into the wilderness for three or four days to fast alone, I'll come back transformed. Presto chango. A new man, a new woman. But what actually happens is something else entirely. There is no miraculous transformation. Instead they sit on their mountain top and the days pass uneventfully. The wind blows; the sun shines; the stars twinkle; the crickets sing. This is all very nice, but where are the goodies?

It takes time to turn water into wine. Jesus could do it with a snap of his fingers. We poor mortals have to kill time, remembering who we are and who we want to be. Then we have to bring all those memories to simmer over a slow fire. The finger snap may take weeks, months, years, even a lifetime.

But it sure doesn't hurt to sit alone with an empty belly among the pinyons and junipers and watch the sun go down.

Memory has an odd way of looking at us when we least expect it. Something that happened long ago, something we had almost forgotten, comes back like a great wind. Suddenly, we are shaking like a leaf in a memory hurricane. Unresolved questions have a way of doing this. Somebody hurt us and we have never forgiven him/her. Or we hurt somebody and we have never been forgiven.

The present goes deep into that closet where the past is stored. We do not forget, especially if the present contains packages we never opened. Sooner or later we have to sit down and pull the wrapping away from the forgotten thing, and stare straight into its eyes.

Many years ago, more than I might care to admit, I was blamed for an unthinkable deed I did not commit. All at once I was the cynosure of judging eyes and words of others, many of whom professed to love and care for me. I wriggled on the needle point of unjust blame like an insect in a specimen box, courageously struggling to extricate myself from the label of "guilty." One by one, my so-called friends fell away. No matter how much I protested my innocence, I was culpable simply because somebody accused me.

Several weeks of hell ensued. I was all alone, fighting for my very career, when the truth came out and the accuser confessed. The story was a fabrication.

I was enormously relieved, and have since forgiven the person who told the bogus story. But "friends" were harder to dance with. Most of them never asked forgiveness. They drifted back into my life, casually as you please, as if nothing had ever happened.

Only today did the memory of that difficult time come back to haunt me. And I realized I was still angry at certain people for forsaking me. Thirty years later! I was astounded, and a little irritated with myself, that I could have let so much time go by without remembering, and purging, the influence of that event in my life.

Thirty years of fermentation. Thirty years of not quite forgetting. Thirty years of associated and related experiences adding to the mixture simmering in the pot.

They say sugar from crushed grapes breaks down into ethyl alcohol and carbon dioxide. Thirty years of breaking down into wine!

But the drug has cleared my head. I can see into people, even those who decided not to like me for a while. I can see, and forgive, their humanness. But I can't get rid of the scar tissue around my heart.

One of the ceremonies we suggest people might perform while they are fasting in the wilderness is called the "death lodge." We ask them to imagine they are dying, and that they have one last chance to say goodbye to those who, in one way or another, played a significant role in their lives. And then they go alone to a special place, to a lodge meant specifically for people in the community who are ready to die. In this place they entertain all those, living or dead, who come to pay their last respects.

In all those years, not a single person has ever suggested that such a ceremony was irrelevant. They recognized the need we all have to die cleanly, without the baggage of resentful or guilty memories. The death lodge gave them a final opportunity to forgive or be forgiven before they went alone to their dying place. Almost immediately they began to remember people with whom they had to eventually engage if they were to enter that passage cleanly.

The death lodge is a memory place, a fermentation place, a karmic place. The people who come to say goodbye are from the past. Though they may continue to play an active role in the life of the dying one, they are nevertheless, at that moment, phantoms from the past. Memories.

When we forgive or ask forgiveness of our memories, they cease to assault us with the same fervor. It's true. Memories get tired of wrestling with us. They really don't like to be ghosts rattling their chains in our bedrooms every night. I think most of them are happy to be told they can stop their haunting and go back to just being memories.

There can be no doubt that Mother Nature is violent. And there is nothing in humans that does not reflect her violence. In Dark Nature, Lyall Watson presents an undeniable case for natural mayhem, perversity, chaos, abuse, etc. All this terrible stuff exists in nature because, in all its forms, it has enabled species to survive and evolve. Apparently, Grandmother gave humans a good dose of it.

It is also true that Mother Nature can be non-violent. She has provided a million ways for species to get along with each other. Much of the time we occupy space with those who we fear most, and often forget, or ignore, the danger. And even when the threat of violence presents itself, we have ways of defending, avoiding, or deceiving. It's not as though Nature equipped us with only a predilection to gobble or be gobbled.

One of the best ways to get along with each other is to be alert to each other. I don't mean live in fear of each other. Fear and violence are sister and brother. We must live in wide awakeness to each other, with the kind of respect that breeds concerned involvement.

While Meredith and I were walking in hills above Santa Rita Flat, I almost stepped on a rattlesnake dozing in the sun. Uncoiled, she looked like a dead stick. We weren't sure she was alive. She showed no sign that she was aware of us as we came in closer. Her tongue never flickered. She never flinched. I stroked her back with a stick. She didn't twitch a muscle. Emboldened, I lifted her tail.

That did it. In a blur of motion, she coiled and struck, her rattle thrashing furiously. If I had not immediately jumped away, feeling that "zero at the bone" Emily Dickensen speaks of, she would have nailed me for sure.

Neither of us were awake to each other. We were both dozing off. And because we were not giving each other the proper respect, a violent episode might have ensued. I am grateful to the rattlesnake for warning me. And no doubt, in her own way, she was grateful to me for only tweaking her tail. But in the heat of the moment, anything could have happened.

Let us walk lightly on the earth, brother and sister, and disturb as little as possible.

If we do violence to the earth, she will do violence to us. Violence always elicits a karmic reaction. When will the blood letting ever cease? Forget the dreams of Nirvana and Heaven. We must survive in this life, this earth. And our children must survive us.

The poison tailings from a mine which has done violence to the earth will bleed into the rivers and the flesh of living things. Mother Earth will exact her revenge against those who wound her. She will take away those very species on which we depend.

Our survival hangs on more than just our technological ways of coping with the poison we ourselves have put into the earth. We will never be able to rationalize the disappearance of our earthly relations. And if, by some random chance, we wind up as sole possessors of this earth, then we will have to start dreaming of Heaven, for indeed we will be living in Hell.

Between you and me there is protective space, a moat, a trench, a fence, a layer of dense air. If you want to invade me, you must cross over that protective space. If, however, you honor this sacred boundary between us, you will not cross without my permission. And I will not cross without your permission.

This holy "betweenness" exists because Nature has given us this much, this right to protect ourselves from each other. She drew a distinct line between us. But she does not prohibit us from climbing over the fence to have a go at each other. In fact, she gave us arms and legs and a brain to aid us if we should so desire.

To violate: "The facilitation of force against another: infringe, transgress, ravish, rape, desecrate, profane, disturb violently." To infringe by infiltrating the boundary. To transgress by ignoring appropriate routes of ingress. There are other means of transgression, equally as violent. They are known by such names as manipulation, regulation, imprisonment, the "law," censorship, propaganda, and so forth. The ways in which we infringe on each other's borders are too countless to mention.

So why does this sacred space between us continue to exist, given our shabby record of transgression? Why do I continue to ask you to respect that space, unless I give you permission to come aboard? Why do you continue to feel the same way? Does this boundary between us give us any hope for survival in the 21st century? Or will we become automatons of violence, servants beaten subtly into submission by masters who assume their will crosses all boundaries?

We must let our memories go back into the dawn of human time. We must ask our sacred ancestors to tell us about the violence in us—and to remember how painstakingly We Who Have Gone Before tended our own space. Then, and only then, can we truly cherish the rightness of the borders nature has drawn between you and me.

STORY-TELLING, COYOTE, ANIMALS

I talked to a man today who wanted so badly to tell the story of his life, his hopes, his dreams. But he couldn't vomit it out because he had been conditioned by his culture to fear ridicule if he did. Growing up in our redneck town, he'd suffered many painful growing up lessons. As a young man, he'd believed in himself as a hero with a mission, with a life story about himself that could have carried him all the way to the ends of the earth. He'd buried his dreams long ago.

Are we no longer the heroes and heroines of our own stories? Are we letting others dictate our visions? Are we accepting the lie that we no longer have access to the dreams that leads to personal fulfillment?

Holy shit! The chariots are rolling into battle and nobody is in them!

Our minds are twisted and hungry from mythical deprivation. We lost hope in ourselves when we accepted the myths a mindless culture gave us. Now our fingers are on the buttons of awesome weapons of self-destruction, and we kill because we cannot think, hope, or dream for ourselves. We have been brainwashed into believing there is no story unless it is someone else's. The more powerful and influential that someone is, the more we seem to want to give our dreams away.

I wish we had at least some young people (or counsels of young people) in the places of power. Some of them have truly earned the right to be there. More than any other segment of our culture, the young are still capable of self-belief. And the music and songs they entertain touch them to the core of their story-telling. The music is total. It rubs against the erogenous zones of their soul. It invokes yearning for God/Goddess. It fills them with an instinctive understanding of the archetypes of destiny, a fate that comes straight from the Holy of Holies.

Contrast the songs of the young with the culture into which they grow via the passage "rites" of constant and protracted social conditioning. No soil could be less prepared to grow them. The only way this

Culture of Lost Personal Stories can feed them is by diverting their attention from their own destiny.

What is the real meaning of life? Surely most of us can still remember that we are mortal, that death awaits us all.

If, with the flick of a switch, I can have a story told for me, why should I care to tell my own? After all, my own story is dull, boring, foolish, and last night I hardly behaved like a hero. How much easier to plunk myself down in front of the television or movie or computer screen and be enthralled, scared, titillated, moved to tears. Besides, who would listen if I told my own story? Who would care?

People who go alone into the sacred mountains of vision return with a story. Yet they are often reluctant to tell it. They say, "Well, I had hoped for something better." Something better? Like angels descending from heaven on ladders of light? Extraterrestrials crawling from saucers? Mary Poppins on a broomstick?

We tell them we want to hear the story. And when, finally, the story is told, it is a real life, a real love, a real dream, a real drama, and it moves us to tears. We Who Have Gone Before weep with us.

Last week, a German woman told her real life story. The last time she saw her mother was in a nursing home. When it came time for her to leave, her mother pleaded with her: "Please don't leave me here. I don't like it here."

It was the last time she saw her mother alive.

While she was alone and fasting, she vividly remembered this incident. For two days and nights she sat alone and felt the memory-presence of her mother. "You've got to do something about this," she told herself. She felt so weak and wretched and guilty.

On the third day, she remembered what she could do. She tottered to her feet and declared, "Mother, would you like to dance?" Laughing uproariously, her mother accepted. Arm in arm, they waltzed across the Inyo Mountains.

A story needs no more than ten minutes to be told. No more than a moment of attention. Yet we rarely have time to tell or to listen.

If we are so tongue-tied, how are we to express our deepest myths about ourselves? How are we to transmit the information that undergirds our survival as a species? For untold thousands of years, we told our stories or the people died. There was no other way to empower each other. There was no other way to learn the song lines. Around the flickering fire, the sacred ancestors emerged and spoke urgently to us of matters involving the whole person. We honored and empathized with the sacred path of our brothers and sisters; we discerned in each other the features of god or goddess; we listed to our place the cosmic scheme of things.

When the young man or the young woman came down from the mountain of fasting and vision, the elders received him/her in council. The elders listened carefully as the stories were told. The stories themselves were valid certificates of incorporation into adult life within the community or tribe. The elders responded to the stories with stories of their own. And they reflected back to the teller the meaning of the mystery as they saw it. Above all, they certified the story-teller to live the life of the story. Their pleasure in the stories of the loved ones lasted for lifetimes.

Where are the elders of the modern world? Do they exist? What are they doing? Are they listening to the stories of the young? Are they finding pleasure in the tales told by those who have come through the passages called "broken home," or "gang member," or "rave angel," or drug/alcohol addiction? Or are they off on vacation? Do they care about the destiny of the people?

But we can hardly put the blame on the modern elders. Have they ever been given the opportunity to tell their own stories?

This summer, the gnats rule. All over the high-country backpackers are hiking out of the mountains, whispering, "Don't go up there! They'll eat you alive!" The Forest Service campgrounds are vacant. Even the most avid fishermen avoid the creeks. The gnats keep rising from the shoreline, like a choking smoke. They invade every orifice, every crevice, every piece of exposed flesh. When they pull away, tiny spots of blood appear, and later, itching welts last for weeks.

Nobody knows why. Some people say, "Last year was a wet year. The critters must have made lots of babies." Other people call them "turn of the century gnats," and talk about the second coming. The biologists are still holding their tongues, trying to identify.

The only person who knows all about the gnats lives down on the Paiute Reservation. She is 96 years old. She can still speak the old language and she looks like a sun-dried apple. She remembers the gnats. The last time they came she was six years old. The great blood suckers arrived like a dust storm and nobody went into the mountains.

The Paiute Great-grandmother remembers even further back, when the elders sat around the fire, talking about the time before that, when the gnats came in 1863, and the elders were themselves youngsters—and their great grandparent elders were remembering that the same kind of gnats had also appeared before the white man ever came, that the best way to keep them away was wood smoke—and that, on one of the 4,000-year-old picture rocks in Coso, there is a pecked image of this very gnat.

We have lost our gnat stories. We have forgotten how things come and go, that at least once in a lifetime we will have a gnat year—and that those satanic pests will exact their due with our blood. We have forgotten to laugh and cry with each other, to heal each other around the fire with stories about blood-suckers and vampires and all the shadowy nuisances of life. We have lost our ancestral gnat-memory.

And then, seemingly without warning, comes the Year of the Great Floods, or the Year of Terrorism.

A story doesn't have to look like a story. I'm reminded of the two-sentence story of a woman returning from the mountain: "I took a big shit," she said. "It felt so good." The elders had a field day with her.

Why is it that we have trouble seeing the story behind a simple declarative sentence, like: "I woke up feeling weak and sick and I wondered what I was doing here" or "I spent the whole night looking up at the stars" or "I remembered times when I was a kid" or "I got so angry at the wind" or "I decided to walk up the canyon" or "I sat all day on a rock."

We often think a story should have a beginning and an ending, that it should build toward some kind of climax. The hero or heroine should confront the fire-breathing dragon or the succubus and then there will be an outcome, a catharsis, and the prince and the princess will find each other. Or we think, "If it's a story, it should move me far beyond my own cursed ordinariness." We forget what a deep river of ancestral empathy runs through our being. We forget to really listen. When we really listen, we see ourselves reflected in the story. We are compelled by our ancestors to say, "Thank you. Yes. How many times have I awakened weak and sick and wondered what I was doing here?"

And we add, "That is a good story. Truth has been spoken here. It is my story too. So be it."

We bless the story-teller.

Many years ago, when my woman and I were working the Wednesday night late shift at Suicide Prevention, we kept getting what was known as a "repeat caller." As I recall, her name was Amy, and she always told a heartbreaking story.

At age 19, she was dying of leukemia. There was nothing anybody could do to arrest the ravages of the disease. Struck down at the onset of a promising ballet career, at first she thought she was working too hard. After a series of tests, the truth was revealed. Three times a week she had to go to the hospital for treatments. Her hair was gone. She had wasted away to an old lady ghost of youthful perfection.

When he realized what was happening, her boyfriend left her. And one by one her other friends fell away. She went back to living in her childhood room in her mother and father's house. Early in the morning, when she couldn't sleep, she called Suicide Prevention. The theme of her story was always the same: Why shouldn't I take my life?

For reasons I couldn't fathom at the time, her calls blinked the red light when it was my turn to pick up the phone. Immediately I knew it was her—a long pause when I answered, "Hello, this is Marin Suicide Prevention." Ragged breathing in the background. Then a tiny, exhausted voice. "Hello."

"Is this Amy?" Another long pause. Then, inaudibly, "Yes."

Once again, I knew my time had come to ponder the most valid premise of suicide—that each of us has the God-given right to remember way back to the beginning how many times we have taken our own life.

At night I dreamed of what I could say to Amy. And in the morning I made love with my woman in the rosy blush of health. What did I really know of death? What did I really know about dying from an incurable disease? I tried to put myself in her place, to feel the icy shadow closing in. I wrote poetry to her. I talked about her incessantly with Meredith. Should I encourage her? Should I tell the truth to her?

"Listen to her," my partner opined. "Just be there for her. Keep asking her questions. Help her clarify her options."

One agonizing night, I played the banjo for Amy and sang songs about love and passion. Anything to relieve her depression.

Then she stopped calling. We never heard from her again. For a while, I wondered what had happened. I combed the obituaries, looking for her name. But too much else was happening on the side. I had begun to take kids into the wilderness on fasting quests. My feet were on the Yellow Brick Road.

But I never forgot Amy. And now, at the end of my life, I realize what happened to her. She died.

And I don't care in the least whether she swallowed those pills or she died with tubes sticking out of her. What's the difference? It's not how we take our life, but how we die.

And every story that has ever been told has the same *denouement*.

Lonely old men tell stories. If you give them half a chance, they'll talk your leg off. How easy it is to avoid them! They sit in the same place for hours on end. They never seem to do anything exciting. And then, if we actually listen to what they are saying, we look into their wrinkles and naively wonder if they have actually experienced the blood and thunder, tragedy and glory—not to mention the tricks and jokes and laughter?

Our old Paiute teacher said Coyote medicine was for old men. Of course, he was an old man. He was the old fart telling stories to the youngsters, laughing into their skeptical eyes.

The old Paiute Indian doctor said to leave coyote alone. He was absolutely right about that. Don't mess with coyote. Don't start feeling romantic about him. He doesn't give a fig for your notions. He'd just as soon tear your eyes out as to act like a cute little dog.

Then why does everybody make such a fuss over him? Don't ask me. I'm sick of coyote. I wish he'd get the hell out of my life. I'm tired of being turned upside down. He always seems to wait until I almost reach heaven. Then he appears to remind me that I'll never get there.

And I can't believe all this fuss American Indian wannabees are making over coyote. It's like their ancestral memory is a sieve. He's been screwing us over from the beginning of human time and these would-bees are wearing coyote tail hats.

Coyote showed up one morning at dawn, just as I was completing a four day fast. Right away, I knew something was wrong. And when he refused the invitation to drink a cup of coffee, I hightailed it out of there. It was already too late. He jumped into my lungs and has been breathing for me ever since.

O Grandfather Coyote, I pray that you will get out of my lungs and let me breathe for myself.

Last night my daughter Selene took me to the hospital. I wasn't breathing well and it seemed like the only thing to do. Trouble was, I couldn't imagine I could make it to the car. I was caught between a rock and a hard place. If I stayed, I would die of oxygen starvation. If I tried to walk down to the car, I would die of oxygen starvation.

Coyote.

One gloomy night several years ago, while fasting in Death Valley, a sudden downpour caught me fast asleep and unprepared. Cursing heartily, I struggled from the sack bare assed naked, without my boots, and made for my pack, which I had left open ten feet away. In blind haste, I fell into a clump of cholla.

Coyote.

Five miles from base camp, at the foot of a steep four wheel grade, I lost the accelerator linkage to the land cruiser. No juice. I gave it the gas. The engine just idled. I crawled underneath the car, looking for the linkage. It was nowhere to be found. I scoured the road backwards

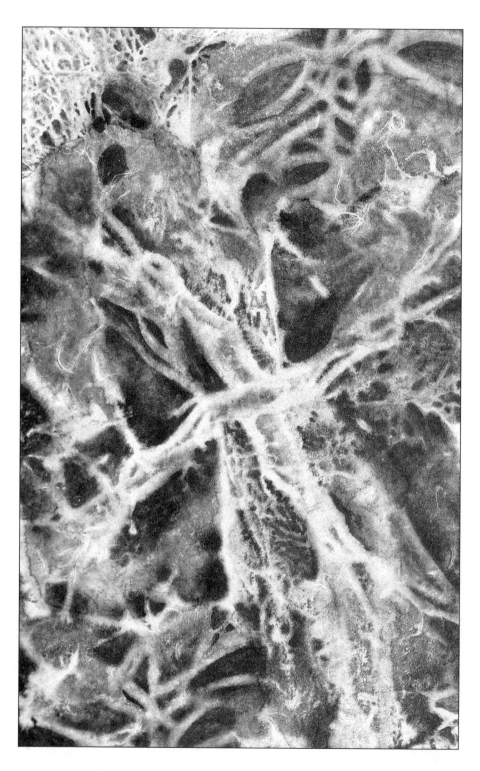

Selene Foster: Photo transfer and mixed media on rice paper, '99

for fifty yards. Nothing. The pit of my stomach dropped out. Everybody up there was depending on me. I was packing in the food that would end their four day fast.

I must have sat in that useless vehicle for half an hour before it dawned on me. The manual choke! I could put the transmission into four wheel low and pull the choke out. Maybe it would get me up the hill.

Before long, the old cruiser was grumbling up the grade at four miles an hour, faster than I could walk.

Coyote.

Three times we stopped the car by the side of the road so that our puppy dog could pee. Three times she ran around on her leash and sniffed here and there but never, even under the most heartfelt urging, did she pee. The last time we stopped, she showed absolutely no inclination to pee and looked at us with pleading eyes.

So we put her back into the car and started down the road. She peed.

Coyote.

When I was in high school, I used to break into the gym with my friends to play pick-up basketball. With a kitchen knife we coaxed the dead bolt back into its carrier. We bragged about how we did it. O yes, we told the story all around.

A year later, when I was a freshman in college, I heard the dreadful news: my little brother had been busted for breaking into the gym. He spent several hours in jail before my parents bailed him out.

Coyote.

He was 17. He was a football, basketball, baseball player at Independence High School, in the little town 24 miles south of us. The local newspaper had written an article about him. The kid was really good. The Chicago Cubs had sent a scout. His fastball had been clocked at 94 miles an hour.

He wasn't a bad student. He had a pretty girlfriend and a lot of buddies. According to his principal, "he was a major presence on campus who always had a smile for everybody." He had parents, stepparents, brothers, sisters, grandparents, and many relatives.

So what got into him and his '92 Mercury Tracer, north of Little Lake, "unknown speed," at 11:25 in the morning? Why did he drift off the highway into the shoulder and skid down an embankment, collide

with a boulder, flip over—and eject through the windshield from an un-
fastened seat belt?

Coyote.

He took the seminar assignment to heart. Shift your shape. It was in Ger-
many, near Breitnau, in the Black Forest. He put a dead fish in a wheelbarrow (a very dead fish) and wheeled it into the nearest gasthaus. He
ordered two cups of coffee from the serving girl. One for himself and one
for his friend, the fish. But when he tried to get his fish to drink, it
wouldn't drink the coffee. Good German coffee to boot!

"Fraulein," he said. "Something is wrong with my fish. It won't
drink the coffee. It seems to be sick."

The young lady expressed regret. "Is there anything I can do?"

"Yes. You can call a doctor. You can find the name of the nearest
fish doctor in the yellow pages."

The young lady made a big show of searching the yellow pages.
"There aren't any fish doctors listed," she declared.

"Well, then, you and I will have to doctor the fish."

"Okay" she said, "but first I have to call home."

She took the phone into the kitchen and dialed the police. "A
man has escaped from the insane asylum!" she said.

By the time the police arrived, the man, wheelbarrow and fish,
were gone.

Coyote.

There appear to be four kinds of Coyote. The first kind is just passing
through. He's crossing the road in front of your car, running away without a backward glance, or way off in the sage, paying absolutely no attention to you. You get a little thrill. "Hey, there's a coyote!" But then he's
gone and life has not changed significantly just because you happened to
see him.

The second type of encounter always involves Coyote actually stopping
in his tracks to look at you. For some reason your presence interests him.

Something in his awareness of you seems to be going "tinkle tinkle," like coins falling into the tray of a slot machine. At the same time, something else goes "clunk," and three lemons click into place. You insert your money—but the payoff goes to Coyote. He gets something on you at your expense. It is not a standoff. He is free to go anytime he wants. So he takes you in and then he trots off. You are left wondering what he is up to. You get suspicious and paranoid. You begin to watch your step. You wonder if you have already made some stupid blunder and tomorrow the boomerang will brain you.

The third type of Coyote is the kind that actually comes up to you. I don't mean those coyotes hanging around the camping areas of national parks begging for handouts. They are more dog than Coyote. I mean the wild coyote who sits down just outside camp for a while, and glares at you—as if he had nothing better to do than freak you out.

If you get this third kind of visitation, hang on. Calamity may lurk dead ahead. You are not going to be able to stop it. On the other hand, you may be in for a wonderful surprise. He will come to you seemingly out of the blue and you will live in heaven for a while. Sudden misfortune, or change in fortune, sudden loss, or gain; death will flip you over to expose your tender underbelly—or death will pass you by so quickly you cannot even begin to imagine its eventuality.

The fourth kind of Coyote is the Dream Coyote, or the daydream Coyote—the fantasy Coyote. This form of Coyote is most familiar with you—and, in fact, can be said to be an inseparable part of you. He is the trickster that is you. He knows you so well you shift your shape to be him without even thinking about it. Some people might call him the Shadow Coyote, for he is capable of such action as you would prefer to keep in the dark. He can steal; he can lie; he can get livid with jealousy; he can get angry enough to kill; he can do nasty things and then promptly forget them. He is one mean mother fucker, and he is you. Me. Us. We Who Have Gone Before.

❖❖❖❖

The Paiute Indian doctor who was our teacher called me on to the carpet one day because one of our people told him Badger was her "power animal." When asked how she came by such a notion, she said she had seen a badger while she was fasting for a vision. When he asked her what Badger had said to her, she said she really hadn't seen a badger, but that she had found a shred of badger skin. That was enough for her. The skin of Badger had told her he was her power animal.

Old Bullet Hawk was pissed as hell. He ranted and raved and said our training wasn't worth the powder to blow it up. Funny thing was, I agreed with him. What did she know about Badger? Why did we think she—or we—had the right to mess with Badger? For twenty years we had been living at the edge of the desert, with numerous encounters with animals in the wild. But what did we actually know about them— outside of identification and zoological books? We were nothing but Howlies on their land, and the old man knew it. Grandpa had nothing but scorn for the white woman from the city who claimed Badger as a "power animal."

No doubt he had good reasons for his anger. Badger was his power animal. When there was healing to be done, he asked the Great Spirit if Badger was the one to do the healing. If Badger came into the lodge, the old man literally became Badger. With his powerful forelegs, he dug and scraped away at the dis-ease in the dark, close heat of the lodge. And even when the old man was ailing with a brain tumor, Badger continued to enter his lodge to do the healing work.

I felt convicted by the old man's scorn. What did this woman know about Badger? What did I?

After a few months, however, I began to feel differently, and actually became upset with the old guy. Why didn't this woman have a right to Badger too? She might have been Caucasian; she might have lived in San Francisco, far away from her European ancestors familiar with the European badger. Cut off from intimate contact with most animals outside of mice in her pantry, cockroaches under her sink, and flies in her food, she might have forgotten Badger.

Even those most deprived of the wonders of the natural world have to start somewhere, for our ancestors will not let us forget that at one time we too lived with Badger in the wild.

❖❖❖❖

Our "pet" dog was brought to the Australian continent 10,000 years ago by traders from the Indus, and was domesticated by the Aborigines. As the centuries passed, she tended to run wild, like the American coyote, and became known as "dingo." The European settlers of Australia domesticated her again, and began to breed her into other dogs, variations of the naturally implanted, instinctual memories of the dingo. In puppy form, she came to us as a wild Aussie Sheepherding-Border Collie-Queensland Heeler Dingo.

As a descendent freely occurring in nature long before humans arrived, our dingo is the sum total of all her ancestors—including the genetic in-breeding of thousands of years of "owners," the ones known as We Who Have Gone Before. She is probably as close as we can get to the mystery of animal nature.

I keep trying to see how my sacred ancestors conspired with her sacred ancestors (and the sacred ancestors of all the creatures in her environment) to breed her. I can only guess at a mystery beyond the borders of contemporary enculteration.

I do not think the mystery lies in our dominance of the dingo. I think the real mystery lies in her dominance of us. No doubt we will have to train her to live with us. But she will also train us to live with her—and she will be largely successful. We will feed her when she is hungry. And if we don't feed her, she will revert to the wild again, and kill rabbits and gobble the decaying contents of the compost pile. She might even turn on us if we try to take food away from her. No, better to give her what she needs.

All of our "pets" are ancestrally wild. They did not stay in the wild because they realized they would be better off dominating humans. You might almost call it a form of parasitism, the way they manipulate us into doing what they want. Better to think in terms of symbiosis. We benefit each other by our association—or at least we like to imagine is so. The young ranch hand in Burns, Oregon, who gave the puppy to our daughter Selene, who then lovingly bestowed her on us, said she was a "cow dog."

Well, I should smile. So that's what she is. That's why we work so hard to make sure she's happy. That's why she continues to do more or less what she wants when she has the chance—to herd humans, little kids, 18 wheelers, back hoes, cows, elk, bicycles, flies, the everwinding white line in the middle of the highway, and blind old ladies with white canes. Sometimes I think we're just trying to survive in the savage world of the dingo.

But only yesterday, in the late afternoon, she started barking out on the porch. Meredith, who had just emerged from the shower, went to investigate. There was a fire outside the house. If left unattended, it would have killed us. Was our dingo bitch looking out for her own interests, or for ours too?

Therefore, I want you to know that our dog is a very special dog. She is not a run-of-the-mill whatever. Yes, she jumps on you with dirty paws and rakes you a mite scarily with her teeth, and cannot quite contain her bladder as she greets you with quivering body and joyously gyrating tail, but I tell you, if you take her into your lap, all 45 pounds of her, you will be transported to doggie heaven. Snorting, panting, licking, thrusting, muscling herself into the most intimate secrets of your neck, she will win you over, or horrify you with the power of nature.

What can you do when you are suddenly transported to doggie heaven? Jump down and run away? Shame on you. The oldest and most beloved companion of We Who Have Gone Before deserves more than this. Accept her salutations. She's happy to include you in her world. And bless your lucky stars you haven't been jumped by a tiger.

Among the mammals and fish that appear to be most comfortable with humans (on the American continent) are: the raven, the raccoon, the coyote, the gopher, the vulture, the sparrow, the dog, the cat, the burro, the bear, the deer, the rat, the dolphin, the shark, the grass carp, and the skunk.

Among the humans who appear to be most comfortable with the presence of "civilized" animals are: tricky ravens, wily raccoons, sneaky coyotes, invisible, burrowing gophers, carrion-eating vultures, nesting-in-many-tiny-crevices sparrows, pack-feral dogs, comfort-seeking cats, spring-fouling burros, hibernating garbage-eating bears, graceful-herb-eating deer, plaster-eating nest rats, wide-ranging-gregarious dolphins, depth-cruising-predatory sharks, vegetation-nibbling grass carp, and skunks who live under barns and emit foul odors. Yes, I forgot to mention the gray squirrel, the scorpion, the black widow spider, the catfish, the starling, the red-tailed hawk, etc., etc.

We adjust to each other. We seem to know each other. A shark swims into our ken. We cry: "For God's sake, it's a shark!" Yet we manage to survive—most of us. Some do not. It is a terrible tragedy to lose a loved one to a shark, or the psychological horrors of a skunk. I wouldn't want to be cut down suddenly (from an angle my arthritic neck can't quite reach), by a red-tailed hawk. We Who Have Gone Before assure me that the humans actually do experience, deep in their memory banks, the fear of such swooping-down-from-above dangers as represented by the red-tailed hawk. Everyone is afraid, except for the stupid ones, of the blind side.

Yet we forgive certain forms of predation, while we hunt down others. Why we do this is a mystery known only to the animal that is us.

The red-tailed seems to be doing well, at least within our range. She caterwauls quite happily in the winds above the alfalfa fields, the open sage brush, the foothills of the mountains, and the upper pinyon-juniper woodlands of our valley. When she comes into town, she does so with a wondrous sense of detachment. Funny thing is, the humans seem to appreciate her. Isn't she beautiful! A fellow predator. Give her space. Let her do her thing.

But the grass carp is a different kind of predator. He comes to us like an alien, hidden away in the fluid deep, nibbling, pecking, digesting the oxygen-seeking algae and aquatic plant life that is stealing the oxygen from the beavers and muskrats and trout and frogs and salamanders and leaches. The grass carp eats plant life. In so doing he saves the mammal life. The hawk eats meat life, and in so doing saves the plant life.

Which way is best? The way of the red-tailed or the way of the grass carp?

Why do you come to me for answers? Consult We Who Have Gone Before.

A great horned owl lives in our trees. She seems to prefer the old black poplars and cottonwoods, where rotten limbs break off in storms, exposing deep cavities eaten away by piss ants, that sink down into the main trunk. She is doing very well on our land, and on the property above us, where the creek twists through willows and birches and stands of wildrose.

She calls at dusk and early morning. *WHO Who who who.* In the late-afternoon light, walking up the path from below, I spy some kind of growth in the branches, a gray cat with sharp ears hunched into its shoulder blades. Looking up at her looking down at me looking up into her soft eyes, I am reminded of Betty Davis as Queen Elizabeth, elegance mingled with something brewed in the underworld by a dominatrix, a predator in an evening gown.

I tell her quite distinctly that she doesn't want me. I'm older and tougher than the rest. I won't kiss your feet, goddess in feather furs, nor will I sacrifice my loved ones. I bravely state, for all the world to hear, that when she calls to me at night, I won't forget to breathe.

Tonight I started to cry because our adolescent bitch, Zorra (Spanish for foxy lady), was lying asleep on the other side of my desk chair. She had enjoyed what we would call a "big day": a 3-mile ramble with M, a romp with a ball, hours of craziness while M hauled fallen leaves, an excellent training exercise with me and the frisbee, and finally, a hearty meal of meat and noodles.

I turned in my chair and discovered that she was there. She could have been somewhere else. But tonight she decided to lie near her "master." For some reason I was reminded of what the Christians call "unmerited favor," or grace.

The day before, we had diverted the creek water back into the lake, which for two months had been drained dry, as we deepened it. Back and forth a backhoe and bobcat had scoured and shaped the lake bottom.

Then we let the deep cavity lie fallow. It was hard to go down there. The empty hole reminded me of death. I felt the agony of all the life we had destroyed with our technological machines.

The excavation appeared barren of life. The trout were long

gone, captured, relocated, killed with stress. Several hundred leopard frogs and bullfrogs and their tads, a half million mosquito fish, and who knows how many hellgrammites, snails, beetles, flies, were gone. The little puddle at the bottom represented the sum total of the rest of the life we had managed to preserve.

And then, just yesterday, with a happy ceremony, we let Birch Creek back into the lake. We were so excited we almost didn't notice the behavior of Zorra, who barked and pranced and raced around the bushes like a banshee, who jumped into the inlet, and let herself be herded back, back, along the long-emptied cavity, by the downward creeping of the little creek against her nose.

Just across the lake, a wild duck quacked loudly. Overhead, a kingfisher clamored, a Coopers hawk skimmed the trees, a bald eagle balanced against the blue sky. And early this morning before we were hardly awake, an owl hooted, a bobcat yowled, and a male blue jay, the "camp robber" who had been hanging around for a month, started screaming an insane imitation of a red-tailed hawk.

The second we let the masculine creek re-enter the feminine lake, all the "spirits" of our little desert bio-system knew about it. There was great rejoicing among the beings of the air. "Amen!" they shouted down from the heavens, "Be it so!" For so long they had watched the lake shrink and the life-giving water flow elsewhere. How well they knew the life giving water trails crisscrossing the land! Even the frogs sleeping soundly in the thirsty mud stirred and dreamed pleasant dreams.

And our dog Zorra? She decided to lie down near her master.

I have long been a student of William Blake. Years ago, I put one of his "Auguries of Innocence" into a song. It was a simple song, chant-like, that went:

> "Wild deer, wild deer,
> Wandering here and there,
> Keeps the human soul from care."

I kept this chant to myself until one afternoon, at Goodale Creek, as the snow was falling and a group of fasters buttoned down for the third night of a fast, a herd of mule deer appeared on the volcanic slope above me. There must have been 30 of them, does and fawns.

I was sitting cross-legged on the tailgate of the old Ford, a bit apprehensive about the turn in the weather because one of the women had gone out with a marginal sleeping bag. But the deer looked so pretty and timid I decided to sing Blake's song to them, just to let them know I meant them no harm.

Immediately, each deer spirit looked up and fixed me with dark eyes. They didn't bolt. They just looked at me. I could have sworn they were listening to the song:

> "Wild deer, wild deer,
> Wandering here and there . . . ."

Inspired, I sang louder. It seemed to me that I didn't look like a two-legged human, but a dark torso and head uttering unusual sounds. The canyon echoed with my hoarse singing:

> "Wild deer, wild deer . . . ."

Then to my amazement, as one, they started down the hill to the truck. They came in so close I could have touched them. They crowded around, the little ones peeking from under their mothers' bellies, peacefully browsing the little sage grasses and the fresh tips of wild rose. As my voice rose and fell with the song, they lifted their heads to listen in rapt attention.

I sang to them until my voice gave out and the snow turned to soft, cold rain. Then they softly moved on into the darkening afternoon, leaving the cracked-voiced old man with a blessing he would never forget.

Since then, I have sung to a myriad of wild creatures. They listened with the same attention as the deer. And never did they run away—with one exception. Coyote.

❖❖❖❖

Surely, the best and most innocent part of me, or you, is like a puppy dog. Bred to work, yes, but even more deeply bred to be a puppy dog. I really want to demonstrate my affection with extravagant gestures, gnaw on bones and fart in complete disregard for the presence of humans, and fulfill all the gross characteristics of my breeding. I really want to live in complete heedlessness to my safety and take what comes with a yelp of understanding. And if I don't admit to having this puppy-dog nature, I'm lost. I'm utterly lost.

Where would I be without a body?

Much of memory is habit. My dog and I know that. She gets so used to our routines that she pines away if I miss a single element of the daily schedule. From the moment I get out of bed, she is ready to go with a day that already, even after only a year of life, has been set up for her by what we are accustomed to doing. If I forget to rough her up in the early morning after a long night of sleeping, she huffily turns her back on me. If I call to her to ask for forgiveness, she acts like she doesn't know me. Then she comes back to get a pat. She always does.

Memory is formed from such bonds. It does and it doesn't have to do with genetic influences. Memory is both nature and nurture. As a throwback to her ancient ancestors, she remembers how to herd, how to nip at the heels, how to maintain borders, how to love her master and mistress. As a creature of nurture, she remembers where her toys are, where she is fed, where the cat is fed, where she sleeps at night, where the cat sleeps at night, what she must do when I am preoccupied with taking my lung medications, how she must behave when strangers come to the door.

What mystifies me is her ability to chase and catch the frisbee. I doubt very much that her forbears had ever known such a thing as a frisbee. Maybe a boomerang, or a stick. But a plastic saucer that hangs in the air like a UFO? This is a memory that the two of us have created together. What's more, she has created habits with the frisbee which I never taught her. She has learned how to grasp it between her forepaws and, with her nose, flip it up into the air so that she can catch it herself. If I don't remove the frisbee, she'd do it all day.

Together we have created a language, both spoken and unspoken. By her first birthday, she already understood "come," "sit," "lie down," "stay," "off," "no," "yes," "good dog," "over there," "where's Mom," "where's Steven," "where's the cat," "where's the frisbee," "good night," "do you want to play," "do you want a jelly bean," "do you want to go for a ride," "dinner time," "walk," etc. And I am learning her language as well. All I have to do is watch her eyes, her ears, her head, the poise of her body, her bark, her play-growl, the little sounds she makes in her throat when the raccoons are into the garbage or the bobcats are stalking the front lawn. Together, we have created a morphogenetic memory field. And if we should be separated, she will remember me, and I will remember her—with the deepest longing.

Stress and Healing

As a younger man, I hardly heeded the wisdom of my body. I made it do all kinds of ridiculous things and didn't listen when it complained. This kind of arrogance is typical of most young people. If the energy is available, use it. There is more than enough. I hooked up my batteries to amazing feats of the moment—basketball, football, track and field, marathons, long-distance hikes. Use it now. Why save it?

When I look back at those years, I see how I was ignoring an even more important theater of energy, one in which my psyche, rather than my body, was the leading player. I wonder how I could have been so doubly ignorant not to realize. I was not only putting my body on the line, but my soul.

Like the body, the soul breathes. In-out. Take in-let go. Whatever is held in (and not let go) has karmic consequences. In my old age, I understand. Breathe in, breathe out. Take it in, let it go. The soul is almost fanatic about this. The soul remembers that it must fly over the cliffs of karma to the sacred nest of eros. It must begin this grand flight as soul and alight as a fledgling spirit.

The body suffers grievously from ignorance of stess.

The phone rings. The person on the other end is asking for my attention, my empathy, my wisdom. I try to compose myself, to "be there." At the same time, my heart begins to pound, my lungs to labor, my body to tense. Without my desiring it, I find myself under the heavy thumb of "stress."

In the old days, I wasn't aware that stress was physical. If I found myself in a stressful situation, I simply powered through, like a hiker in deep snow. As I recall, I even welcomed the challenge of stress. "Aha," I would say to myself. "This is a psychological situation. This is no threat to me. I can handle it easily."

Now I handle stress as though it were an unopened package that could very well contain a bomb. My psyche goes on the alert. There may indeed be an abyss dead ahead, lying directly across my path. My hands tremble. My breath goes out of control. I am forced to dance with the contents of the package.

I have to open the package anyway. My sacred ancestors tell me there is no other way.

Stress affects the breath. When we are under stress, we breathe faster. Our hearts beat faster. Our bodies go into states of alert. Mostly, we are not conscious of this reaction. We go ahead and deal with the situation, with whatever is focusing our attention to a tiny burning hole in the fabric of consciousness. The way we focus involves a kind of dance with that which is stressing us. We dance in close, we dance away, we engage, we separate, we try to keep from being whacked too hard. The object, of course, is to end the stress, to still the heart, to re-focus the breath.

My doctor describes this dance as enantiodromic, a back and forth pulling and being pulled between the body and the psyche. He calls it a "vicious cycle." I agree. Stress tends to lead to greater stress. The energy goes back and forth like a ping-pong ball until one of the two players goes in for the kill. Of course there are ways of alleviating stress, but inevitably it will come back to haunt us—in the form of bodily illness and the natural processes of aging.

What is it within us that is so afraid of running out of breath, of suddenly keeling over from a heart attack, or developing some kind of ailment that grows stronger and stronger until it does us in? Should we find recourse to modern medical chemistry, which rightly says: "Your state of stress could very well be caused by an hereditary and/or chemical imbalance?" Or should we elect to go into the stress, to live through it like a pilgrim in a labyrinth, to give ourselves to a psychological journey of re-generation?

How much is physical? How much is memory?

I cannot answer. All I know is that as my body undergoes more and more pain, my psyche remembers, ever more clearly, that my life course has always been deathward.

And I wonder, why should the prospect of dying be depressing?

Selene Foster: Mixed media on paper, '99

We can start with the ultimate in Judeo-Christian healing. Jesus, the ultimate medicine man. Shaman extraordinaire. But who was he? Jesus the man is irretrievably lost in the mythology surrounding him.

I want to know about Jesus the man. The only way I can understand the healer is to know the man. But Jesus the man has been censured out of existence. The "faithful" have destroyed any evidence that would suggest that Jesus was really a man like other men. If he had to be a man, reasoned the Council of Nicea, then he had to be unlike every other man—a god.

Okay. So the Christians tell me I can't be like Jesus (even though he asked me to be). And I can't do what he said I should do ("Go ye therefore and do as I do.") And all these ancestral feelings that tell me I can heal, that come to me from thousands of years of life and death, mean nothing if I don't follow the advice of the Council of Nicea: "You must go to Jesus to be healed."

So I have stuffed any fantastic notion that I could be a healer. And regardless of all this, people come to me to be healed. But Jesus' "mortality" is the only thing I can imagine, now that I am facing death. I must turn to face my own destiny. My knees are shaking and I don't know what to do or say.

"If the fool were to persist in his folly, he would become wise." (Blake)

My doctor is a small Japanese-American man with a moustache and a sudden grin. Most of the time he is quite in earnest. But I have learned how to make him laugh. I tell him something unexpected, like, "Doc, you are a sweetheart." He breaks into a grin and immediately gets serious. But I know I've touched him in a soft place.

He rarely talks about his private life. I know he has a wife and two children. Growing up in a Japanese-American family after World War II, he couldn't have had an easy time of it. No doubt it was very important to his ancestors that he become someone with whom they could be proud. I know he graduated from USC medical school. But that's about all the goods I have on him. I wonder where he grew up; what kind of childhood he had; how he lost his cherry; where he did his internship; why he came to live in this remote valley. Once I wrote him a letter inviting him and his family to visit us in our wonderful lakeside home. He declined in a very professional manner. I wonder how many other invitations he has declined.

The fact is, Asao (for that is his first name) has given his life to healing. He is a "shaman"—but never will he be given such a name by the western medical tradition that called him. And, having taken the Hippocratic Oath, he does his best by it. No doubt he is a fallible man. I have never known a doctor who wasn't. That's why I love him in spite of himself, and honor—though not always obey—his advice and prescriptions.

My New Age friends consider me to be ill-informed and culture-bound. They remind me of the healing traditions of naturopathic, homeopathic, allopathic, herbal, holistic, Chinese, charismatic, and pagan medicines. They remind me of all the spotless gurus and healers who were on top of it all, who channeled the spirit. God bless 'em, they send me pills and treatises, statistics, and advice on alternative methods, some of which I heed. But most of my "faith" in healing, as it were, remains focused on Asao the man and the depth of his professional empathy.

He's *my* medicine man. I can live with his way. After all, he was recommended to me by a woman, an excellent M.D. in her own right, who once fought beside Che Guevarra and the Liberation Front. He just gives me the facts, as he knows them. Then he tells me what I have to do to stay well, or prevent sudden death. He knows I'm going to die someday. Yet his entire reason for being in my life is to keep me alive and productive. I can always count on him to be full of advice and a problem solver. A body guard. I can always respect where his prognosis comes from. Medical fact plus delight in personal skill plus intuition plus prescription plus caring. An adequate foundation upon which to build a healthy psyche, mind, and spirit—and upon which to build a healthy death.

I think what I like most about him is his openness to new ways of seeing how he can be more effective. When it occurred to me that I might have a rare, genetic lung disease, he immediately had me tested. His research into Alpha1 antitrypsin probably made him the only expert in this disease in our valley. I can depend on him to know, and if uncertain, to find out.

Asao is not going to get carried away with his patients, no matter how he might feel inside. He is going to be a professional shaman. But when I die, he will be there with me, and I will feel his love for me, his care. I will say, "Asao, I saw you one day walking across the street in the crosswalk in front of my car. You were looking down at the pavement. In the posture of your shoulders I could see how you carried the illness of the people. I knew that I was one of them."

Then I will ask him about the Land of the Rising Sun and We Who Have Gone Before, the "we" who reminded him he was a healer.

Whenever life looks too depressing, I go to the desert for healing. So what if I have to tote my oxygen pack along? I can still appreciate nature with a tube up my nose. The extra time modern technology has given me can be put to good use.

Only now can I appreciate the plight of the handicapped, or the aged, who are forbidden vehicular access to most remote areas within national "wildernesses" and "parks." We can't get very far away from a road or a telephone. Nevertheless, there are still a few places (near sea level) where I can go and find solitude within a reasonable distance (for me) from my car: Eureka Dunes, Breadman Canyon, Horse Thief Canyon, Confidence Hills, North Death Valley Wash, Soldier Pass, Old Dad Canyon. As I've grown older, my appetite for the far away and exotic has been replaced by an acceptance of my own limitations—and a corresponding love for whatever natural space and time I can still access.

I get out of patience with those who must pilgrimage to "power places" on the earth. They tramp all over kingdom come only to discover that what they are looking for has always been hidden inside their restless souls. Just give me an acre of solitude, an afternoon along a cut bank, or a clear night under the desert stars. Don't make me do anything. Just let me be.

There is a special place in Death Valley up by Keane Spring, a test hole blown by a gold-thirsty miner a hundred years ago into the side of a limestone hill. A scar. It reminds me of my father, who once blasted a hole into a hill looking for gold. When I sit there I can see out over the cattails and willows crowding the spring. As the night comes on, the wind quiets. The barren peaks on the western horizon darken against the mauve fingers of sunset. Pallid bats flit silently above the willows. A poorwill calls. Everything is still.

I will go there someday, and I won't have a tube stuck up my nose.

I first became aware of the healing power of the creosote many years ago while fasting in the Eureka Valley. It must have been 100 degrees in the shade, and I had a touch of heat prostration. Early in the afternoon, I sought shelter beneath a large creosote bush, lounging in the shade as the sun moved around it. I must have dozed off in the late afternoon. When I awoke, a down-canyon breeze had sprung up, and I was looking up at the sun through the snaky branches. In tune with the wind, the shadowy patterns were singing across my body.

For a long, long moment I felt an enormous sense of well being. It seemed I had fallen asleep in the Paiute sweat lodge and Grandpa was waving his eagle feather. The whooshing of the feather through the superheated air had awakened me to the coolness of relief.

At that moment, I realized the creosote was aware, that it was remembering me, and giving itself to me and mine—to provide shade for the weary traveller—home for the jumping mouse—food for the chuckwalla. How blessed it felt to be remembered by all the Creosotes Who Have Gone Before.

❖❖❖❖

There seem to be two kinds of people. Those who heal themselves alone in the dark chambers of their hearts; and those who heal themselves by wearing their hearts on their sleeves. The introverts and the extroverts. The former use deep, untold secrets as healing sources. The latter use the revelings of deepest secrets as healing sources. I am one of the former, but I have learned to respect the latter.

If we feel led by soul memories to become, in one way or another, helpers in the healing of others, then we must see how it is with the one who has come to us for healing. How does he/she carry her secrets? How much or how little guidance is needed to guide him/her? And what will he/she do with the guidance given?

Many there are who, in the hope of being found, feel compelled to reveal their deepest secrets. But the deepest secret eludes them, budding in the dark cliffs of forgetting like a perfect crystal. It is that to which we must guide them, cutting through the smoke screen of verbalized feelings. We must help them discover the resources they can from within.

And many are those who keep their feelings to themselves, who live so deeply in the pride of self-motivation that they cannot see their need for others. We must guide them to the doors against which the sunrise surges, flooding their secret chambers with the love of others for them. We must help them reach beyond the dark shield to seize the most mature precept of human law. "No man is an island, entire of itself."

Never underestimate the power of the vision fast to spin the wheel—to take us on a bee line straight for the mysterious flowers of love. In the face of such healing power, we hardly need to do anything but watch.

BEETLES, GHOSTS, COMPUTERS, WORMS

I was sitting alone in the Confidence Hills (Death Valley) on the third evening of a vision fast, thinking about what it meant to have a terminal lung disease, when a darkling beetle bumbled into my range.

I just happen to love stink bugs. They remind me of the tapping beetles of South Africa, the ones the bushmen considered sacred messengers from God.

So this fragrant creature came up to me and I decided to have a little chat. I poked at him with a twig. Immediately, he stuck his rear end up in the air and farted—which is what stink bugs do to offend predators.

Determined to push this fellow further, I touched his front paws. Immediately, he rolled over and lay on his back, legs stiff in the air, dead. If I'd been a raven, I could have gobbled him on the spot. Yum, yum. Stink bug.

But stink bug just lay there. I watched him for a long time. Dead as a door nail. My conscience began to get the better of me. "You killed him." "You scared the life out of him." I poked him with the stick again. No response. Lifeless as a pebble. All at once it was time to pray for stink bug. "Dear Grandmother, don't let him die. I was only kidding. I didn't mean to kill him."

And then something else caught my attention. It could have been a moth, or a bat, and my awareness of my surroundings changed. I was off on another train of thought, another journey through memory. The moment couldn't have lasted more than a few seconds. When I looked back at my victim, he had vanished.

I guess it is just human folly to finally look away and get lost in an unrelated matter. I felt pretty small then, no different than any of the other species that predated darkling beetles. Fooled by a stink bug—distracted by the surprise of killing him so easily! When I had him on the ropes, he played his last card, the most powerful of all—the memory that predators wouldn't necessarily kill stink bugs if they thought them already dead.

We humans call it patience. Biologists call it the instinct to "freeze."

Total vulnerability in the face of death breeds patience—especially the kind of patience associated with hope. Be patient. Fake it if you have to. And if you get the chance, run like hell.

Beetles compose the largest order in the animal kingdom: twice the number of species of the next highest order, Hymenoptera. Many of them are downright ferocious, like the Tiger Beetle, which stalks and pierces its prey with sword-jaws. The larvae are just as bloodthirsty as the adult. I don't think I would want to be so small as to be this beetle's prey. I account myself lucky to have been born human.

But then I wonder about my luck. They say humans have few predators, but everywhere in my environment I see potential danger. Does this mosquito sucking on my skin carry malaria or encephalitis? Does that tick, clinging to the dog that just bit me, carry rabies? Will that rattlesnake upon which I am about to step, strike me with poison? Will that hive of "killer bees" swarm me? Will that unshielded sun give me skin cancer? Will that bolt of lightning choose me? Will that tornado smash the poplar through our house? Is that water pure enough to drink? Will that car coming at me lose control and whack me out of existence? Will that thug take my wallet and then my life? It goes on and on—the freeway bombers, the dark alley lurkers, the jealous lovers, the gang bangers, the serial killers, the child molesters—all the viruses of nature. At almost every turn there lurks a tiger-beetle of the natural/human variety.

How could We Who Have Gone Before escape the fear of death? And now we, their descendants, are in even worse shape. Down in the basements of our cunning rat-holes we fear snakes, gophers, and moles.

By the same token, how does any species, in this voracious universe, survive? It would seem we all keep remembering to live—and we keep forgetting, or trying to forget, the constant presence of death. We traipse along without a care in the world and Wham! The Deadfall Trigger flattens us.

Tiger beetle, violin spider, bark scorpion, kissing bug, rattlesnake, bacteria, virus, earthquake, I know you exist. I know I should watch out for you, and I do, sometimes. But most of the time I don't even want to think about you. Granted, you will probably climb into my bed some night while I'm sleeping.

I'll have to deal with you then.

Every spring, at our "upper campus" along Big Pine Creek, our groups have to put up with swarms of lady bugs. The meadow grasses become a rippling, shifting carpet of orange.

We sit together in a circle and talk. Meanwhile, the lady bugs explore our skin, invading the most tender secrets of our bodies. No telling how many there are. They seem as many as stars in the sky. But you can't be romantic about these sweet little bugs, no siree. They're in your hair, your nose, secreting tiny specks of a bitter, amber-colored fluid supposed to have a toxic effect on vertebrates.

We merge anyway. We get used to the pests. We extract them from our crotches without a thought.

Of course, lady bugs have another persona, that part of them that remembers they can only survive if they eat aphids, mealy bugs, scale, and mites.

Tomorrow I will drive up to camp with a pail and a net. I will bring home a few hundred thousand lady bugs to our peach trees, which are dense with aphids.

Yes, I will be altering the eco-system. I'll be separating, transplanting these aphid-eaters from their local biosystem. Maybe I'll upset the balance of nature along Big Pine Creek. Maybe aphids in greater numbers will invade the birches and willows along the creek. Maybe, horror of horrors!, there will be a decline in the lady bug population. Because I have chosen to transplant lady bugs to a different ecosystem, I am hardly less culpable than Coyote, who captures seeds in his coat and conveys them to a different range.

We all seek to make our homes fruitful. The nest of a sparrow is no less fruitful than an apricot tree. Are humans any different than the dusky-footed wood rat? Why?

One evening in the desert, I saw a woman watching me from a nearby creosote bush. When I approached her, she vanished.

"Who was it?" I later demanded of the spirits. For a long time they were silent. Then the answer came.

"What you saw was memory."

"Memory?"

"Yes. You saw memory trying to become real."

"My memory?"

"Not necessarily. Many people have been there before you."

"You mean they leave their memory behind?"

"Yes. Pieces of it."

"But memory is invisible!"

"On the contrary. Memory is visible everywhere in the physical world."

There was truth in what the spirits said. The land we live on is covered with memories of the past—our trees, for example, some of them planted 100 years ago by people long since dead. The very house we live in is held together by nails driven by the hands of men I don't even know. Against the walls hang pictures and photographs staring out at me from the past. The shelves of my study are filled with books, all of them written by the ghosts of yesterday.

Everywhere I look, I see pieces, parts, flecks, reflections of times gone by. I am surrounded by palpable reminders of the memories of others.

I go outside. Encompassed by the bewildering multiformity of nature, I am dumbfounded. Memories everywhere. Nature is nothing more and nothing less than living things remembering to take their forms, their place, their function, their fate, in the cosmic masquerade of corporeality. In every living thing I see the ghosts of those of the same species who lived before.

I begin to wonder if, in fact, all of nature isn't ghostlike, an expression of invisible spirit. The seed tops of *artemisia vulgaris* nod in the autumn wind. Yes, even the wind carries the memories of former winds, and is what it is because of yesterday, the day before yesterday, and all the way back to the beginning of wind-time.

Who was that mysterious woman who watched me as darkness fell? Was she a reflection of my own memory? After twenty-five years of putting women out on fast, she could have been just that—one of those women, or all of them rolled into one—memory trying to become real, to plant itself in the ground, to become a living soul—a vision faster looking wistfully at base camp.

Or was she a reflection of someone else's memory? This seems entirely possible too, for many women had fasted in this same area down through the years. And when it came time to go, a piece of them, their longing to be here in that place, in the vast, empty desert, never left the locale, but lingered, longing for a way to become corporeal. All at once, there was a way. There was an eye to see them, and a memory to remember.

An acrylic painting by Emerald North confronts me every time I sit behind my desk. It is a rare and striking work of art. It was created from Emerald's memory, which remembers the look of trees, branches, sun, and sky as her ancestors have remembered them. The painting itself is a ghost, a shred of sunrise infused by the imagination of millions of ghosts from the near and distant past.

As I grow nearer to death, the entire world I live in has begun to assume a ghostlike appearance. All these bundles and complexes of memory wandering around, trying to attain some kind of ultimate form. By "ultimate form" I do not mean just the body. What my body is trying to become is simple enough. It is trying to remember how to be cold, stiff, and lifeless. Eventually, I will find a way to fulfill my destiny of corpselikeness. Maybe the way will lead through the heart, or through the brain, or through the hardening veins. Maybe memory will discover a weakness in the lungs, or in the soil of the flesh, where fantastic, death-dealing creatures mushroom like cancer. Are we all physical ghosts attaining the reality of death?

And how about the psychic ghosts, the soul ghosts, the invisible complexes of memory banging about the world like excavated mummies, the ones who are half in love with death because their memory tells them death holds the secrets of immortality? O, I will be one of those!

My soul is sick with love for Eros. I waste away into soul-likeness. I forsake the past—even the present—for the future. I want to meet my lover face to face. I want to make love, to be revived, regenerated, relived. I do not want to pass into nothingness.

I walk the main street of my home town. I wave cheerfully at everyone I know. They look at me, the waving man, and they are reassured that life stays the same, that life is for the living. But I think to myself, life is not my goal. They are ghosts.

Yet to some of them, I am a ghost.

To me, the mind is the most puzzling mystery of all. I have always loved the mind, even though I was never much of an intellect. Mind was more like experiences I sought, often to the utter dismay of reason.

For a long time I wandered the earth attempting to recover from this malady of "rationality." Then I discovered why. In the first place, I didn't belong in the ivory tower. I wasn't about "to perch upon a golden bough to sing to Lords and Ladies of Byzantium of what was past, or passing, or to come." Like Goldmund, the artist, I wanted to live and bleed in the here and now. I wanted to go out into the streets where the beggars rubbed elbows with the damned. I wanted to stand my ground before the rotting corpses so that I could write a poem. It wasn't reason that gave me back to myself and my heart's desire.

I am fascinated by Gregory Bateson's definition of "mind." I want to scream at people. "Don't you know that the mind is not the brain? Don't you realize that the way to mind is the passage from childhood to adulthood? Don't you know that the way to mind is through the soul?"

It wasn't the brain that got people through thousands of years of war, famine, and plague. It wasn't the brain that raised and nurtured and initiated children into adulthood. It wasn't the brain that controlled the passions, tempered the violence, and schooled the senses. It wasn't the brain that sought to be one with the laws of the universe.

It was the mind. And don't you forget it.

I was a teenager by the time our family was baptized. The Reverend De-Sagher led us down into the baptismal font, and in front of the whole congregation, dunked each of us three times in the holy water: once for the Father, once for the Son, and once for the Holy Ghost. When it was over, I didn't feel particularly redeemed. I felt embarrassed and confused by what had happened. The Holy Ghost had not come down like a tongue of fire to consume me because I was one of the chosen ones. Instead, I felt as exposed as a drowned rat, ashamed that the congregation could see the outline of my penis through my bathing suit.

I didn't lose interest, however, in the idea of a Holy Ghost. Of all the teachings I received at the Valley Baptist Church, the Holy Ghost was by far the most compelling. According to the New Testament, the ghost fell in fire-tongues upon the true believers at Pentecost and everybody started speaking in different languages.

How dearly I wanted to be one of these flaming-tongued ones!

It was not to be. I would never be possessed by the Pentecostal Holy Ghost. I did go to fundamentalist "revivals" where many around me were swept up in a kind of mass hysteria they called "possession." They fell down on their knees and repented and declared themselves to be spontaneously healed. Some of them even spouted the gibberish of "tongues."

Like I say, it didn't happen to me. I could only watch with a sort of critical awe born of feeling separate and alone, an outsider, an alien. The babbling ones seemed to be accessing something very old within themselves, an altered state similar to the drug induced frenzy of the Sibyl at Delphi—but they needed each other to access it. The vast majority of them didn't seem to be able to do it alone.

My own experiences with the Holy Ghost have been occasioned either by the ingestion of a psychedelic substance like LSD or mescaline, by fasting in solitude in the wilderness, or by giving/receiving love in intercourse with my woman. Invariably, the feelings that have come over me have been related, within my own perspective, to creativity. Suddenly I am able to see with inspired insight, to peer into the very essence of things. I seem to be remembering with the accumulated intuition of my sacred ancestors. The memories don't last. Why should they? As long as they do, I feel chosen, special, and honored above all men.

I can understand what Coleridge meant when he described the ecstatic state of the solitary artist:

> "Weave a circle around him thrice,
> and close your eyes in holy dread.
> For he on honey dew hath fed,
> and drunk the milk of Paradise."

And that's why I love the painting of Vincent van Gogh, William Blake, and Emerald North. They were painted by the Holy Ghosts.

I can't even begin to understand the manipulation of computer memory. I know the secrets are accessible to me, should I want to learn them. But somewhere along the way I decided that I would not become an initiate. Nevertheless, I call my hard disk "Atriedes," after the royal name of the doomed duke in the ecological science fiction novel, *Dune*.

Mine is not a particularly up-to-date or expensive computer. But it does the job, and is doing it at this very moment. When I tell it to do something, it remembers how, and does it. In this sense, it is a usually reliable extension of my own memory. I remember the word I want, and then I remember how to type the word on the keyboard. The computer does the rest. It imprints, in Garamond, the word on an electrical grid, and remembers how to arrange the word with other words. Then it remembers how to select and print the word on paper.

Nevertheless, Atriedes is no better than my memory. It serves my memory. It can only remember what I decide to commit to it. At least that's what I tell myself. Nevertheless, something in me is not certain who serves who. Though I depend implicitly on its ability to remember what I tell it, there have been many times when the doomed duke shut down completely, and forgot everything. Everything!

At such times, I have to become the computer's victim—and savior. Without me, the memory of the splendid duke would die forever, and Paul Atriedes, the son, would never accomplish his messianic purpose. So I take appropriate measures to restore, revive, or reconstruct the computer's memory banks. Or, despairingly, I give of my own substance and buy a new computer.

I, Duke Atriedes, will never give up. I cannot give up. The computer will live on in my sons and daughter. And if I have to exit this book, I will die by exhaling a deadly virus from my rotting teeth directly into the lungs of those Harkkonens who seek to use technology for evil purposes.

The old goat can learn a few new tricks. After all, there's nothing in the software that was not there from the time our ancestors climbed down from the trees. It's like any other discipline. First I do this, and then I do this, and this, and this, and if it doesn't work out, I do this. Gradually I master sequences and interrelationships and symbols. Before I know it, I can send and receive electronic letters.

The benefits of this discipline are well-known. Unlike the telephone, which rings at the most inopportune times, you can talk with people at your leisure, and compose a reply in your head before you actually reply. In this sense, electronic mail is more "literary" than the telephone. Instead of saying it, you write it.

We must never underestimate the power of the written word. It has a kind of finality to it that ordinary conversation could never reach. And when you multiply that power by the number of people who can be reached instantaneously by the simple click of a button, you have at your disposal almost unlimited literary access to the masses. Which is not to ignore the access of the masses to you.

We are free to decide when to write or to read what has been written to us. Nevertheless, there are drawbacks to this freedom. If everybody decides to write to me at once, then I am overwhelmed with letters that require answers—and inner tension, due to overburdened memory banks, increases. Spam can do this. How the hell does it get my address? On the other hand, I grew up on spam during WW II. It was all we had.

Some say that the computer age has speeded up our lives. This certainly can be true of our social lives. On the other hand, the age of speeded-up information can be left in the dust by anyone who goes to the sacred mountain to live alone for a few days. Such intervals in our lives make us aware of even quicker methods of communication—like the wings of prayer, or songs of forgiveness and love, or faster-than-light speed connections to the spirit world.

Nothing compares to a mild evening sunset at mid-winter, the trees outlined against the vermillion golden western horizon. You'll never see a picture like that on the Internet. If you're not there in person, you're not there. Sure, you can be virtually there, get your cheap thrills, but it's not the same as being there. If you don't believe me, go out into the real world alone, just like you pretend to do in virtual reality. Sit on a stone beside the road, like I just did, and surrender yourself to the real. Something is stirring in the bushes behind you, but you can't quite see because it's getting dark. Maybe it's a mountain lion. Maybe it's a mouse with huge jaws and voracious teeth. There is no virtual gear to remove, no technology. There is only you and the mouse and the darkening west, a misty moon, and a billion mysterious worlds hanging in the sky.

We can leave the small computer field (linked to our own species) and enter the giant computer of the real. We can link ourselves to all beings. Everywhere, connections, communication, information, intelligence. Everywhere, memory. Then we bring what we have heard and said back to our cramped little consoles and hemorrhoidal chairs, armed with new insights, memories. And maybe our souls have a little more room in which to maneuver.

There are those who claim this new technology is soulless. I do not agree. With the deftest touch, soul infuses the electron with the power of love.

Computers don't change anything.

"Arrakis exists to train the faithful!" exulted Paul Ma'dib, heir of the house of Atriedes, having led the Fremen into victorious battle against the forces of the evil empire. Paul is the savior, the messiah, the prophet, the son of the doomed father. His mother, the witch-goddess Lady Jessica, eats the spice and drinks the poison of life. Possessed of Bene Gesserit powers only women can truly appreciate, the mother largely determines the destiny of her son.

My computer, a temple to genetic memory, was built by the fated House of Atriedes. From this house will eventually come a savior, a prophet, a leader against the forces of evil. This prophet will be a son of the father, the original prototype. But his (our) fate will be determined by the mother, the goddess, the witch lady, who lives in the memory of We Who Have Gone Before, the women who mothered, grieved, nurtured, and inspired, who drank the transformational poison and gave away their fondest dreams, yea, suffered living death, in order to know the secrets of the future.

Have enough of the faithful been trained by our beloved Earth? Does this bastard offspring of Atriedes (technology) and its consort the Bene Gesserit witch (ancestral magic) stand a chance to realize our messianic purpose?

The 21st century lies before us. The denouement is unclear. The outcome will depend on the memories represented by the Lady Jessica, the memories that go back, way back, to the beginning of life, to that confluence of gasses and proteins in a dirty comet's tail from which we came, screaming for information and an evolutionary future.

The binary code. You hit that particular button, the memory registers plus. Everything else is minus. If you tell it to remember some thing, it will remember only that thing. Nice and pat. Hardly a substitute for mouse memory, but useful.

I'm reminded of the great white pelican who migrated south from Canada with all the other pelicans, but then decided to turn aside from the ancestral path to spend the autumn on a lake in Ohio. Nobody in those parts could remember ever seeing a pelican on that lake before.

But pelican survival was optimal. Humans crowded around the edges of the lake to throw bread crumbs and to marvel at the sight of a crazy pelican getting fat and lazy lakeside. But just about the time the water began to freeze, the pelican arose, circled the waters of the oasis, and flew due south.

Pelicans are born with much more than computer memories. They do not always behave according to either/or. Nor do humans. If we were only true/false, we never would have survived. On our long migratory path to the present day, we did unpredictable things. We clicked false instead of true. We remembered indefinite places. We paused here instead of there; we turned aside now instead of then; we jumped when we should have crouched; we ran when we should have fought; we fought when we should have taken cover. Every time we did the unpredictable, we learned something that was later remembered. And so we evolved to our present state—plus or minus.

No matter how the nations and the races seek to maintain their precious borders, the iron bars are already gone. The old sacred cows have come tumbling down—especially the information that kept us from reaching each other's lives.

If a tree leaf is a creation of treeness, then a computer is a creation of humanness. Treeness and humanness are both quite natural. Both store up memories of We Who Have Gone Before.

A tree does it more gracefully, eh?

A message arrives on Atriedes to tell me a worm has invaded the internet. If it isn't a worm, it's a virus. Worm: "serpent, dragon, reptile, creeping limbless member of the genus Lumbricus; endoparasitic helminth; larva of insect, maggot; spiral tool" (ODEE). In Latin, *vermis*. In Lithuanian, *varmas*. Worm as varmit, or vermin. Worm as snake in the Garden. Worm as parasite. Worm as larva.

Is anything in the universe impervious to worms? From apples to Apple computers, from dirt to interstellar dust, there's always a wriggler somewhere. And if it ain't a maggot it's a virus or a bacterium or a black hole or a loophole. In *Dune*, the worm was an evil gene in the Atriedes ancestral tree. Faulkner, Joyce and Dickens' novels are filled with worms like these.

A worm in the internet? Fascinating, but an old story. To paraphrase Blake: "The invisible worm that flies in the night has found out thy memory, and thy secret life it doth destroy." Memory worms, viruses, maggots. I'm reminded of the poetry of Baudelaire, and the parables of Kafka and Poe. Larvae can hatch in the webs of our most precious memories and god knows what kinds of monsters might come forth, beating dark wings against our so carefully built passageways of rationality.

Even as I write this book, I am living with a worm that came into my computer a month ago, and began gnawing away on my files. Some of my favorite paragraphs have disappeared—almost as though the ravenous little creature considered my best writing to be the best eating. Having suffered the loss of some of the tastiest parts of myself, I am now learning how to thwart its appetite with certain key strokes at certain moments. Sometimes I wonder if this worm is any more conscious than me. At best, it seems to be a standoff. The varmit will have its due.

We live in such a linear fashion! Our precious plans are mapped out from here to there, on a straight line, like a flight plan. From Los Angeles to Denver. From Denver to New York. Departure and arrival such and such. Or take Interstate 15 to Reno, then Highway 395 to Mammoth, etc. We don't anticipate much trouble getting to where we want to go. But it doesn't always happen the way we want it to happen. A suicidal terrorist is on the plane, and he wants to go to the Twin Towers. Someone ran through security and all flights were cancelled for three hours. The landing gear light didn't come on. The tail section is wobbling. The car is acting like an old horse who can't pull anymore. An oncoming motorist with one too many beers in his brain is about to stray over the white line. Your stomach is reacting wildly to something you ate last night. You can't keep your eyes open after staring into the windshield for ten hours. Suddenly, the linear becomes vertical.

Another name for "worm" is "coyote."

Another name for worm is death. The earthworm feeds on decomposition. Even so, computer memory decomposes into syntax, numbers, symbols, and electronic impulses. Decomposition. Born alive in order to die. Some forms last longer than others. But they all arrive at the same end. Worm bait.

Like my social security number and my passport number and my driver's license number. Like my code word on the internet or my medical insurance number, or my address or telephone number. Gibberish. Worm payola.

Energy equals mass times the speed of light squared. All things die. And then their replacements die. Entropy is all. Entropy is wormfood.

Selene Foster: Photo transfer and mixed media on rice paper, '99

TEACHERS AND ELDERS

A man came to our school to study wilderness initiatory rites, a therapist from the east coast, married with two children. He was a good man, a quiet man, and he looked like John Lennon.

Well, this man was walking down the main street of Big Pine and two adolescent boys started following him, taunting: "Hey, fag! How about a butt fuck?" Now this same man had fasted for four days and nights on a mountain in the wilderness, protected by nothing more than atmosphere and the clothes he wore on his body. That same man had traveled to the remote jungle home of a South American *curandero* and had studied with him, living like a savage in a bamboo house at the edge of a crocodile-infested swamp. This man had been places these kids would never go. He had fought with jaguars and boa constrictors in deep, drug-induced trances. He had known the most intimate mysteries of his woman's body, and had assisted in the birth of his two children. He was a man, and he was a teacher.

Still, he flinched a little at the ignorance of these boys. Sure, they were uninitiated adolescents, but even little kids had no right to say such things to their elders, no matter how different they looked.

It seemed quite obvious to him that these boys lacked midwives. They had never been initiated into manhood. They had never been truly tested to see what they were worth. And they would probably never face such a test—unless life brought them the requisite challenges and they were intelligent enough to recognize these growth-events as tests of manhood. These tests teach us that no man can ever be judged by appearance, that self-worth can only be won in the murky corridors of the labyrinth.

What is even more obvious is the fact that our culture lacks teachers for the young. Real teachers. Not math or English or Science or Home Economics teachers. Rites of passage teachers. Elders. Birthing into adulthood midwives. Men and women who care about what is happening to the young, who want to turn them into men and women. Initiators.

The group was about to enter the sauna. She ran back to her car to get a towel. In the squaw grass near the creek, she stepped on a coiled rattlesnake. The fangs caught her just below the knee.

The night before, she had sat beside Tinnemaha Creek, in the starry darkness, and tried to listen like the Buddha for what the river was saying. She had lingered there for hours, trying to make sense of all those burbling voices, finally returning unfulfilled to her tent and disturbing dreams.

She told us she had not felt connected to the spirits. Her mind had wandered. When she tried to bring her attention back to the creek, something rustled in the bushes and scared her. She could hardly sit still. When her story ended, she told us she "felt unworthy."

She returned with her towel just as we were taking off our shoes. "I want to complete my story," she said calmly—but her eyes were wild. She pointed to the fang marks on her leg, her face draining with shock.

We tied a constriction band just above her knee. I squeezed as much blood out of the wound as I could and sluiced it with water. We waited to see what would happen. Maybe the snake hadn't envenomated her. She sat down abruptly. "I feel a little woozy," she said.

We drove her to the hospital, 30 minutes away. Better not to wait. But by the time we reached the ER, it seemed obvious. She had not been envenomated. No swelling or discoloration, hardly any pain. Two hours later, the doctor pronounced her whole. "You were lucky," he said. "It could have been really painful."

Later that night we talked with her. Yes, she said, the bite had indeed completed her story. She was, after all, connected to the wild. Her connection point didn't necessarily have to be a river. Instead it had been a rattlesnake.

Connection—the essence and the object of teaching.

Long ago, rattlesnakes sprang from the memory of Mother Nature. Why mother rattler remembered that humans could also live in a rattlesnake world is her business. But I think she wanted to teach humans how to be careful—and, above all, to bite without envenomating.

❖❖❖❖

I was never a very good student in school. Sure, I could cough up what the teacher wanted. But something inside me always rebelled, wanting to be somewhere else than in the classroom.

When I became a teacher at the university, I experienced the same difficulties. I felt restless, bored, and self-disbelieving. I was always glad when the bell rang.

What I didn't realize was that I was a child of Nature, and that I would only be happy in the wild. Now, looking back at 30 years of wilderness work, I wonder if my destiny in life was simply to sit at the feet of Nature.

Bred in the suburbs, educated in the city—surely, I was a child of human culture. What am I doing out here groveling in the dirt, watching bats flitting about in the gathering darkness? Another night alone, defenseless, with nothing to eat. Another night looking up at the stars.

Nothing exists in our world that does not, in one way or another, teach us. Not that we are always aware enough to catch the lesson. Usually we're sound asleep. And we must watch out for people who tell us they are always awake. Many of them are high on speed.

How many times have I been whacked by circumstance, just so I can wake up and see what's really going on? At age 63, I'm a little punch drunk. If the universe has taught me anything, it is how dense I am.

Nevertheless, something else is growing within me, something that seems to be the result of living—and learning—through all those years. You mustn't laugh at me when I say that the growing thing is the realization that I am somehow special, that my life has been significant, at least to me, and that I, of all people, should not have to die.

Maybe you feel this way too. Maybe not. Who can fathom the stirrings of immortality within the soul? Immanence of death seems to bring it on. I look around at the natural world. Everything perishes. I will too. Why should that make me special? Am I some sort of ego-maniac?

What is the teaching of Nature? Where do we go when we die? Does our Mother forget us entirely, or does she re-member us somehow, in the image of what we were becoming? You tell me.

We look back on our lives and remember our human teachers. Most of them have melted into the background. A few stand out. No need to try in the moment to remember them all. Usually they come to us when we least expect them. That is, their spirits come. Something they said or did jumps into memory like a rabbit running across the road. We turn into the skid and remember.

At that moment, we learn something that effects our behavior. Sometimes the lesson is bitter. Sometimes it is endearing. Sometimes it fills us with resolve. Never do we pay it no heed.

At such times we are deeply thankful for our teachers. No doubt, we should be equally thankful for our ability to remember.

❖❖❖❖

Older folks have lived the longest; therefore, they have accumulated the most memories. It stands to reason. Wrinkles equal memories. Surely wrinkles, creases, sags, and mottles can teach us young'uns a great deal about our own destiny.

But nowadays, old age is hardly "in style." Every once in a while you see a movie in which an old man or woman enacts the role of "wise teacher." A few of these films have enjoyed astounding success—such as Obi Won Kenobi and Yoda in the Star Wars anthologies or Professor Dumbledore in the Harry Potter series. Usually, the wise one is a magician or a sorcerer. But not always. Evil old men and women are almost as prevalent as the good and wise ones. Consider the vile, ancient witches in Macbeth, the evil old man behind Darth Vader, He-Who-Must-Not-Be-Named in Harry Potter—the old hags and warlocks who inhabit modern horror movies, lusting for blood and thirsty for revenge.

Elders-in-the-real, like the ones in our lives, are also portrayed on the silver screen, but all-too-often they are nothing but empty shells devastated by family secrets, desiccated by guilty memories, like Faulkner characters or decadent Prustian sensations. Where is the wisdom of the elders? Does it exist only in the digital memories of young writers who want nothing more than riches as they grow older—but surely not so "older" as to die of cancer, heart failure, emphysema, or varicose veins?

Is the wisdom of the elders in music? Ah, how could we ever forget the enchantment of Billie Holliday, Ella Fitzgerald, Blind Lemon Jefferson, Robert Johnson, Joan Baez, Tina Turner, Eric Clapton, B.B. King, Charlie Parker, the aging Madonna, Bob Dylan, Leonard Cohen, or the wrinkled virtuosity of the classic soloists on violin, cello, trumpet, sax, guitar, piano, banjo, drums, amplifiers. No doubt the elders speak to us in music.

Does elder wisdom appear in all the other arts? Don't ask me such tomfoolish questions! The muses crave the seasoning of age. They would rather fuck an old saint than a young wannabe—not that they don't also lust after the young'uns who already see. But youth is only one half of the pie. The other half is mind and spirit. Mind fermented in the blues, and spirit up against the wailing wall.

Are the "elders" of our time also capable of teaching wisdom to our age—those oldersters who have led seemingly "ordinary" lives, like having babies, competing in a hostile male world, sinking into the despair of alcohol, drug-addiction, separation, and divorce, surviving the quagmires of love, parenthood, illness, and depression? What about the elders who adventured/endured over 50 years of seemingly uneventful marriage?

Those who have lived long always have something to teach us. Age carries its own rewards. The wisdom of these rewards does not always seem appropriate to our life path at the moment, and all-too-often is considered to be "conservative," or "irrelevant."

How foolish we would be to ignore the natural processes of aging among humans, the way death's approach tempers and changes us. I am reminded of an old man in the same Assisted Living facility in which my parents lived. He had been a chauffeur to Clark Gable, a camera man for dozens of Hollywood films, a companion to William Holden, and a lover of Capucine. Dying of cancer and liver disease, he held himself with pride and dignity, and even though his political views were somewhat to the right of John Birch, his appreciation of the last days of his life touched everyone to the quick.

Likewise, my parents, who lived ultra-conservative Evangelical Protestant lives, had something to teach the young 'uns with green hair, hiphop, and Ecstasy. One didn't have to listen to their words to see the rewards of 63 years of marriage. And their innocent pleasure in little things was touching to anyone who allowed him/herself to accept them. Again and again, I found myself touched to the quick, despite all those thunderstorm years I spent individuating myself from them. And I wondered if it would ever be possible for there to be a cultural/educationally sanctioned way to bring the young and the old together—not necessarily within the family setting, where sometimes bitterness, resentment, and habitual living inhibit deep communication—but within a formal, councilesque setting where everyone has their say and no one owns the complete truth.

Early in their lives, the young must come in contact with death. Not as some abstract concept, but as the corporeal reality of which they are an inseparable part. They must be taught, without morbid implications, that they too will die, and that the gradual process of rotting, called "aging," gives off brilliant flecks and sparks of mystical insight. No doubt they can be helped to see and hear the pitch of death-wisdom in their music. If our educational process could do it right, the young could be "educated" to see that it is their own death that fascinates them, that this very fascination is what lures them into true maturity and will kindle their desire to die a good death.

The elders know. But they have been prima fasciously ignored by a culture in which "growing old" is not the way to live. O.K. So *Rolling Stone* is really all about making *dinero* and keeping its considerable holdings—with all those precious individuals, families, life stories, hopes and faiths—secure. No blame. The elders did it for God knows how many centuries. And if *Rolling Stone* needs to make money, so be it. Nevertheless, I wonder, where are the elders of *Rolling Stone?* Where are the elders in the State Department? After all, they are both in competition for ratings.

Nobody in high political and media places recognizes how they and their own kind age and die. If they do, they don't want to reveal the secrets for fear "popular approval" will plunge.

Give us elders. Give us hundreds of thousands of elders willing to take a stand, willing to hazard their own self-righteously held value-wagers on the spinning wheel of fate. Give us hundreds of thousands of elders who were put out to pasture before they had completed their life-long visions of service, who still have something important to tell the lovers they will soon leave behind. Give us hundreds of thousands of elders who are able to disregard the hypnosis of the corporate media in order to tell their truth. Give us hundreds of thousands of elders who use their power to bring back the rites of passage to our floundering culture. Give us hundreds of thousands of elders who faced death and came out peeing in their pants, who changed clothes and began to speak with lightning honesty. Give us hundreds of thousands of elders who get sick to their stomach when everyone around them begins to wave flags and shout about American pride. Give us hundreds of thousands of elders who are willing to hobble bravely into the sinkholes of ghettos and barrios to bring a tremble and a balance to the neighborhood cradles in which they live.

Give us elders who, in their youth, gave themselves to the infinite seductions of their bodies, who in their adolescence, faced the darkness of an uncertain future, who, in their adulthood, accepted the discipline of winter's responsibility, and who, in the springtime of old age, came forth from a lifetime of labor to live not only for themselves, but for their children and their children's children, and for the lost children of grandmothers and grandfathers everywhere.

Elders legitimatize each other. They recognize in each other an essential memory-force enabling humans to survive as a species. But they have been set apart—or have they set themselves apart—from the main currents of the human river, and even though they faithfully exercise their rights to vote, most of the time they feel disenfranchised. They play golf, bingo, cards, gossip games, watch TV, and lament about what is happening in the world outside their safe enclaves. Yes, times were better, or at least saner, when they were younger. But does it really matter whenever or wherever we have lived? Hard times have always come and gone. Yet the elders traditionally have raised their voices together in meaningful dialogue.

What knowledge, what power, what force do the elders possess that has been absolutely necessary to the continuance of human life? If they have given it as mothers, fathers, sisters and brothers, they possess the god-power of love.

Elders are far more faithful about voting than the young. Why? Are the young far more cynical and despairing than the aged? Or is it that the young simply refuse to accept what their elders claim to be the only political-economic "state-of-country" for which to vote? Why are the young so afraid to speak out in some way that will alter the "reality" of their elders? In the 1960s they did it by sheer unvoting numbers. They sent a message that could not be ignored. If, in fact, the young no longer choose to vote, then how will they make their version of truth overwhelmingly obvious to the elders? Will they simply buckle under and do what their parents' generation tell them to do? Will they find a way that avoids the violent connotations (in almost every country) of peaceful protest against obdurate establishment? Perhaps the young will forsake the immediate concerns of their bodies and reactive emotions and childhood resentments and, networking together like a billion Christmas lights, rise like a bright shadow into the reluctant acceptance of those who profess to guide them.

It all seems to come down to the values elders hold. Some elders are openminded. Most are not. I speak only about what I know of my culture, which is geared mainly to the values of white people. An overwhelming number of elders are other colors, other shades. Because I was born white, I have not gut-experienced the values of non-Anglo European cultures. If I had, I would be far more revolutionary in my rhetoric.

What I do know is that the elders of most cultures want the best for their people. The luxury-dependent whites are no different than the poorest elders in death-ravaged Afghanistan. We want the best for our own. If my granddaughter is threatened by terrorism, I will resist with an alert love. Monsters move among us. And if my Palestinian granddaughter is threatened by American-made rockets, I will resist with an alert and angry love. Monsters move among us. And if dim-witted zealots threaten to ravage this earth, my granddaughter's only home, I will resist with all the love and fury I still have at my command. For monsters move among us.

We elders want the best for our people.

Hospice: "house of rest." In Classic Latin: *hospitium*: "hospitality, lodging." (See "hospital": "asylum for the care of the sick").

"Host," the root of "hospice," is one of the most fascinating words in the English Language. In the ODEE, "*host*," means "army" in Old Hebrew: "a great company." A large number of people. In Old Latin, "*hosti-s*" means "stranger" At which point the reader is referred to "guest," which is also related to *hostis* (enemy, originally "stranger"; whence *hostipot, hospit*; "guest host"). In other words, the word "guest" is related to the words "enemy," "stranger," and even the word "guess." One more twist: in Old German, "guess" is related to the word *geist* (ghost.)

So where are the elders who welcome the "host," the strangers, the "enemy?" If in fact they are about to die, why do they tend to be so inhospitable to "the innumerable host who lies down to pleasant dreams?" Friends die. Enemies die. Strangers die. Guests die. The "host," so that we might live again, dies. In giving hospitality to their own kind, the elders gain secret power, unknown to the quick and the young.

What is ahead for the host of the earth? What role do the elders play in the great drama of the home stretch, where all living creatures face the finish line? Only We Who Have Died Before know the full prowess of dying.

Evil and the Higher Self

I must begin any discussion of evil with the recognition that evil exists in humans as well as in nature. I do not know evil apart from nature. And I cannot see much difference between human evil and natural evil. The human rapist is no different than the male scorpion fly lying in wait to ravage the unsuspecting female. Rape exists in nature. So it exists in humans.

Murder is no stranger to nature. In the frenzy of their ecstasy, and not without premeditation, the female tarantula and praying mantis kill their mates.

In a frenzy of jealousy, a trance of dissociation, or the cold fury of revenge, a man kills his wife. What's the difference?

If this destructive tendency exists in nature too, do I have the right to label it with the human word: "evil?" Do I have the right to conjure up lurid pictures of the "devil," or "Satan?" Maybe, if I absolutely have to see it that way.

But any discussion of "evil" comes down to imaginary differences between nature and human. What right do humans have to call nature evil? If, in fact, nature is an indivisible amalgam of "good" and "evil," then am I not also good and evil? Or goodevil?

Through the eons, while our genetic memory was aborning, we never once escaped the fact that death, destruction, genocide, rapine, etc., dwelt in life, and in our evolutionary path. We can remember eons of peace. And we remember eons of war. As we grew up in our lives, the idea of "evil" was no surprise.

It would have been very easy for me to choose to live a life of "evil." In fact, there were times when I consciously chose evil, or what seemed to be evil, in order to find out what evil was all about. I couldn't stop myself from being curious. I wanted to clarify those "forbidden" spaces where my memories were vague.

What surprised me were all those people who were afraid of

evil—afraid of seeing it in themselves—such as those Hutus who killed 50 fellow Rwandans per minute. They were deeply afraid of evil. To keep from looking squarely at the terror in themselves, they projected it into an "enemy," a "traitor," a "poison," a hated Tutsi.

What a fool would I be if I pointed out the evil in others and didn't point it out in myself? There's nothing weird about beating your breast and crying, "Woe is me!" What's weird is saying "Woe is me" because everyone else is a sinner. This latter attitude causes all the problems—which is not to say that there isn't a similar attitude in other animals. I refer you to Goodall's famous studies of the chimpanzee.

Nature—human nature—is quite capable of running amok, of killing indiscriminately. If you try to hold yourself back from this fact, and consider yourself to be above such base actions, you run the risk of blindly following the next pogrom, the next purge, the next genocide, the next Hitler—or even the next American President.

Humankind is capable of the most extreme forms of natural evil. However, this tendency does not seem to have been built into us as completely as it has into many other species. I am fascinated by this distinction. It may be that nature's memory has provided for a kind of human flexibility regarding "evil" behavior.

I would like to think so. If nature is evil, then nature is also altruistic—i.e., "good," as opposed to evil. Watson's *Dark Nature* contains many interesting examples of natural "altruism." We have observed many instances of munificence in dolphins and whales. This kind of altruism is quite typical of the human species as well. In fact, humans derive a great deal of pleasure from remembering altruistic heros and heroines in our history and mythology.

Apparently, it is just as important for our survival to act for the good of all, as it is to be self-serving. For every Nero there is a saint. For every Bin Ladin there is a Mother Theresa. Though I am not qualified to speak of the biological reasons for this ethical flexibility—to be as open to "virtuous" as to "evil" compulsions—I am certainly qualified to speak about myself, and my own experience.

Years ago I stopped to pick up a hitchhiker ("altruism"). The young man who got into the car turned out to be knife-wielding maniac ("evil"). He would have killed me if I hadn't figured out a way to reason with him. The only way to was to go into his psyche, to see myself from his perspective. "Good" can do this. (Evil can too). There I was, looking squarely at the cutting edge. I saw his mother, and I saw how she controlled him. And deceptive words (evil/good?) leapt from my mouth as easily as rain obeys gravity. I spoke to him in his mother's voice and controlled him by tweaking (ever so slightly) the conscience his mother had instilled in him. I tricked him with lies.

Even now, as I look back at this incident, I marvel at the ability of the good to be insightful, intuitive, and sneaky. And I marvel at its power. The Native Americans called this power "coyote."

This same power resides in all of us, even in those who are unanimously considered to be evil by every one around them. They possess this power as well. They may be unaware of it. They may even revile it, stamp on it, do their very best to eradicate it. But it lives in them like a memory. And if the right buttons are pushed, they remember. The memory may be dim, hardly conscious, but it will stir them. Maybe they will not be stirred enough to be deterred from their evil course. Those who are completely focused on the power of evil are not likely to be suddenly dissuaded by the good. But something deep in most of them will be moved—the memory of good. For a moment they will not be completely evil.

I could write a book about evil. So could you. We know it in ourselves well enough. If we don't know it, we're in trouble. I've watched crazed killers break down when confronted again and again by the awful fact of what they have done. Some don't. A few are so controlled by a need to maintain some kind of personality in the face of overwhelmingly gruesome memories that they "can't remember," or they remember only that which maintains some kind of self-constructed picture of themselves. Most of us would be quite willing to admit that there are plenty of evil memories running around in the shadows of our psyche.

I'm not referring just to memories of things we have personally done. I'm also talking about tendencies, about reactions and attitudes buried deep in our consciousness that jump out at us under all kinds of provocation.

The mass media gives us provocation all the time. Its entire preoccupation is with eliciting knee-jerk memories, and no distinction is made between "good" or "evil." With a few well chosen words, the commercial network "news" can stir up anger and hatred toward certain "suspected" individuals, regardless of the actual truth. Without thinking, we are animated by memories of murder and rapine as old as human history. Our hearts beat faster; our adrenalin count goes up. All at once, we are in favor of bombing that horrible beast ("Kill the bastard!")—and the same goes for anyone innocently connected with him, including women and children.

Five minutes later, all our sympathy, all our love and care, goes out to the family left homeless by a fire, or who have just lost a family dog. We dig down into our pocketbooks and give of our substance so that someone we don't even know will survive bereavement or destitution. Without knowledge of any of the circumstances (maybe the husband beats his wife and children; maybe he is actually a crook; maybe the parents are hooked on heroin), our memories of love and caring are teased out of us like a symphonic conductor evokes the violin section.

Many of the people of America, like the people of any nation, have suffered horribly down through their history. Ethnic genocide, slavery, civil war, suicide, terrorism, and violence of all kinds. Possibly the worst has been the systematic exploitation of the very environment that has sustained us. All and every experience of such evils has become a part of the memory of every American, particularly those whose ancestry is "native" to America. It saturates the land, and we are composed of the stuff of the land.

No less than anyone else, I have been manipulated by We Who Have Gone Before, whether for "good" or "evil." Given the number of pirates and outlaws in my ancestry, I am surprised that I have not given myself even more completely to the experience and expression of evil. Nevertheless, I can't keep from jumping like a little dog through certain flaming hoops my memory dares me to attempt.

Without a thought, I find myself imagining unspeakable cruelties to another person. This often happens on the highway, when someone cuts me off, or forces me to react in order to save my (or their) life.

Just the thought that an accident caused by somebody else might occur is enough to set me off.

If, in fact, I cannot deny such emotion-memories in myself, how can I deny them in anyone else? On the other hand, if I cannot deny the "good" in myself, how can I deny it in anyone else?

Evil is remembering—remembering that I, and everyone else, is evil. Good is remembering that I, and everyone else, is good.

What I do with these memories—how I let them affect my behavior—is totally up to me. Personally, I am deeply drawn to those stories, those myths, about the asshole who goes through a dark night of the soul so that he can be transformed and rescue the people and the land, from evil.

New Age people like to talk about such things as the "higher self." Beautiful people with names like Sunshine Ocean and Shakti Nirvana and Storm Eagle tell eager millions how to access the "higher self." As I listen, I consider the terms I have set for my own life. I would never have qualified as a New Age guru. It has always seemed to me that the "higher self" was something I earned by dint of despair. My spiritual side did not magically appear just because I decided I would channel God.

I've listened carefully to these gurus. It could very well be that I miss quite a bit. They stand so tall and beautiful and always speak from a place of knowing. Every day, every minute, every second they seem to be in touch with their higher selves.

Of course, I know nothing of their off-stage lives. I just know I'm not like them. I flood rugs with my vomit and flush my shit down toilets and keep hoping that somewhere along the way a God or a Goddess is waiting to forgive me. I get up in the morning. I look into the mirror and see my sagging face. Do I consciously think that God is staring back at me? Try it yourself and tell me. God is there, yes, but so are the old age resentments of the Devil. I wonder if the gurus experience the same kind of dilemma. Apparently, they have transcended it.

I would love to spend a few days living the completely private life of a guru. I would love to hang out in his or her bedroom, or bathroom. Do they pig out on chocolate? Do they watch TV? Do they live "politically perfect?" Do they masturbate? How many feet of toilet paper does it take to wipe their ass? Do they actually shit? Do they actually drool in their sleep or get off on pornography? How do they look when they get up in the morning? Do they wonder if rasty odors are arising from their genitals? How often do they take a shower? What do they eat for their breakfast? Do they smoke pot? Do they medicate themselves with chemicals? Do they drink Single Malt Whiskey Scotch from the finest distilleries, or do they buzz on beer or wine? What do they say to their loved ones at a picnic? What do they eat? What do they do with their garbage? Does the higher self clean up after them?

As I've aged, I've had to live with accumulating memories. Through all the blundering I can see my own version of a sacred path. But the trail was blazed through the dense, dark jungle, and most of the time I was overcome with the demands of the moment. I wielded a dulled machete against the tangle and roots of memory, which always were in the moment—now. And always, in the darkest jungles, guilt grew like a kudzu vine.

I made some headway. I didn't actually get to where I was going. I just kept hacking away at guilt, grief, fear, loss, and routine, and sooner or later I came to a clearing, where I met my higher self. I was overcome with feeling and faith. But I couldn't stay in the clearing. There was always work to be done. And I wasn't any better at holding on to my epiphany in the clearing than most other blokes.

People who came to me to be "healed" might have been disappointed that I was not Soaring Hawk or Leaping Dolphin. I was just a human being, with all the weaknesses and karma of a sinner. Through nights of great travail I agonized over my mortal condition and my inability to be what was expected of me, to be a healing medicine chief, a wielder of higher forces that would transform others. I did what I could. I worked hard. I cried the tears of others and shed my own. I prayed and prayed and always felt unequal to the prayer.

Higher self? Forgive me for saying this, but to me the higher self lives in the keenest center of memory, right at the core of the darkest feelings, down there in the rankest, foulest wound. I cannot tell you how to get there—except to say that memory is the way to get there. I cannot say, "Live in the sunshine." I can only say, "When you get to the end of the rainbow and find only rain diamonds that melt in your hand, don't stop believing in the obvious. Somewhere in the vicinity you will be nudged by another rainbow."

I'm sure that my higher self dwells in my corpse. I know this because I have looked at many corpses, and in all of them I have seen my higher self in a beloved body that has returned to the earth. That's why I think there's something fishy about people who always claim to be dwelling in their higher selves. They seem to be distancing themselves from that "lower" part, as if these nether regions were not connected to the "higher." Something in me persists in thinking that the higher agrees with the lower, and the lower with the higher.

I gave a good part of my life to investigation of the lower. I consorted with criminals, prostitutes, outcasts, and indulged my "baser" urges, the lusts and hungers of the socially forbidden. But never did I encounter anything that was not connected to the "higher self." Never.

God was in the tramp. Spirit was in the murderer. The goddess smiled at me in the eyes of prostitutes and laughed from the faces of criminals and perverts.

Surely, if there is an Almighty, would He/She require us all to take the high road? I find it hard to believe that there are people who walk the high road with both feet. They may be as deluded as the sinner who reasons that he/she is wholly lost. And who are we to judge who is on the high and who is on the low? Like the rest of creation, we walk both roads at once.

A line by Roethke comes to mind:

> "The lowly worm climbs up the winding stair."

Surely we have as much right to memories of eternity as earthworms.

❖❖❖❖

I want to discuss those who do terrible things in the name of the "higher self." Yes, there are just as many who do good, but at the moment I'm more interested in those "moral" and "ethical" types who will go so far as to kill, imprison, or degrade in order to fulfill the destiny of their "higher selves."

On second thought, I guess I don't feel like talking about them. After all, they were the ones who killed Jesus, Gandhi, King, and all those millions of people who didn't see things their way.

When I read the New Testament I am astounded at how often Jesus expressed his deepest anger at Pharisee hypocrisy. Again and again he went after them. He saw in them the face of the true enemy. They were the ones who judged others because they considered themselves holier and "higher" than the rest.

He fought a losing cause. The "higher selves" got him in the end. But he left a few choice words behind, preserved forever in our memory of The Parable of the Pharisee and the Publican:

> "Everyone that exalteth himself shall be abased;
> and he that humbleth himself shall be exalted."

Hypocrisy must be a memory strand in the human morphogenetic field—in which I live, in no higher standing than anybody else.

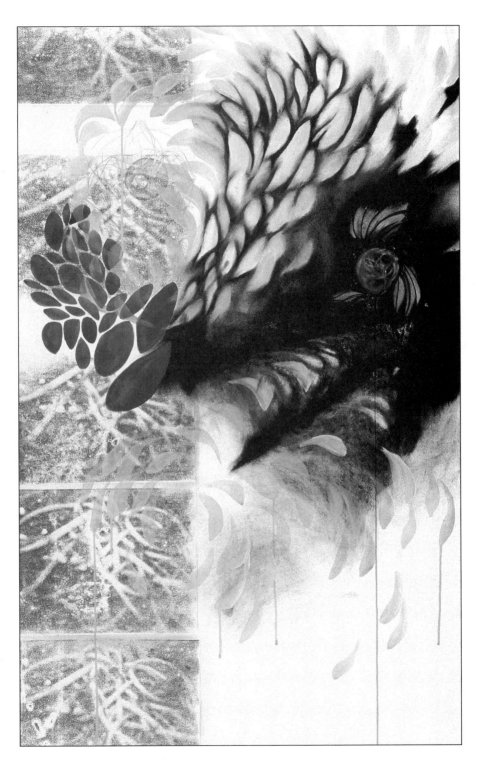

Selene Foster: Photo transfer and mixed media on rice paper, '99

Solitude in the Wilderness

Whenever I go alone into the desert, I am most aware of being in the act of remembering. The mountains, the rocks, the bushes, the beetles, the birds—they all belong to this remembering. To be sure, the body plays an important role as an agent of memory. The memory cells of the body extend to the skin, the neuromusculature, the genetic cellular structure, the blood, the gasses breathed in and out, the brain (especially the hypothalamus), and all the other physical characteristics of the human morphogenetic field.

Let's take a walk through the desert with our bodily memories. The day is hot and clear, with a soft breeze blowing up the canyon from the valley below. A wren sings from a nearby creosote bush, a lonely sound punctuating the hoarseness of our own breathing. The way is uphill, through a wash. Strewn with granite boulders, the trail disappears altogether, and we find ourselves scrambling, tripping our way upward, against the mountain. The heat prickles our skin. We stop beside a creosote growing precariously in a crack between the rocks. Sweat stings our eyes and creeps down our necks as we look up the canyon in the direction we are travelling.

Perhaps it occurs to us that we have found our way thus far by remembering how to use our legs, where to place our feet, how to balance to avoid slips and falls, when and how to breathe. And it all came to us automatically, like a faith. The breeze carries the memory of cool water to the sweat oozing from under our hat. We remember sensations of deliciousness and shivering. Muscles tremble in our legs, and we remember work, exertion, tension, effort.

The resiny leaves of the creosote limb brushing our face are remembering too. Year after year they have been stirred by the wind and sun, bent and numbed in the unrelenting cold of night, released and relaxed under the dictatorship of summer suns. Now they quiver ever-so-slightly in the near-proximity of our body, which lingers within their memory field like an odor, a taste, a noise, a touch, a commotion. We share memories with the creosote, for we are both physical bodies.

But we are hardly aware of our sharing with the creosote bush.

Our minds are somewhere else. We're remembering something from our lives—a moment of triumph or defeat, a word, a phrase snatched from conversation, a thought or idea that has been niggling at us all day.

Nevertheless, the creosote has given us something. We take it in without a thought, without being aware. We have become a little more like the creosote. Our human memories are tinged with resin; our bodies are hardier, more whiplike, more rooted to the desiccate soil.

But what about the creosote? What about the rocks, the birds, the bugs, the air, the mountains? What do they gain from being with us? This is a far more difficult question to answer. The scientist would laugh at any attempts to answer it.

I think I make a difference to the creosote. For a moment, I occupied its space—a large, (relatively) noisy being who did not object to its presence, who, in fact, hardly noticed it. I think the creosote is aware, however dimly, of the physicality of this sweaty thing, and remembers, in its trance-like existence, a relationship with the human—a bond, a communion of shared mortality.

I wonder if the network of animal, vegetable and mineral that we call "the mountains," remember humans too.

We live briefer lives than creosotes. Out in the Johnson Valley (Mojave) there are creosote clone rings more than ten thousand years old. These sentient beings die from the inside, like the hole in the middle of a donut. But they keep growing out, replicating themselves with such exactness that there is no questioning their memnonic powers. They remember themselves so exactly that they can give birth to perfect copies of themselves.

Now this ability truly interests me. If they can remember so well, would they forget us? After all, we've been brushing up against them for thousands of years.

Everything in nature remembers us, even as we remember everything in nature. Without this memory, none of us would have survived, none of us would have remembered each other. Without memory of each other, we would have become extinct long ago.

The psychology of solitude has occupied my attention for over 40 years. But I am too great a lover of the desert to be objective about what I have discovered. There is something in me that always wants to be left alone so that I can remember.

The act of remembering pleasures us. Invariably, it opens a path to the future, and shows us a way to go ahead.

We remember so that we can heal ourselves.

No wonder the prophets and saints and heroes and heroines and medicine people went alone into the wilderness. When it came down to it, they could not get what they needed from other human beings. They had to go alone into the silence of God, Spirit, Mother, not simply to seek answers to the dilemma of human mortality, but to heal themselves.

Healing (in natural solitude) comes from remembering. There is time and space to do nothing but remember—looking into the distance or examining the dirt under our bootsoles. In natural solitude, we can call on brothers and sisters for help.

We have not lived like saints. Our memories are not all sweet and radiant. When we go out into the wilderness without food, shelter, or company, we often go to dance with the demons of our past.

We heal ourselves by being honest about these demons. We don't try to ignore them because we would be fools to do so. And if sometimes a memory forces us into a deep, dark place, we go willingly— not to chastise ourselves, but to savor, to see what we can learn.

Learning is one of the most important functions of memory, and certainly the most healing.

I am sitting on the ground looking out at the desert. I know that everything I perceive is only a part, an extension, of myself. As such, it takes on the color, aspect, and quality of my memories. If what I remember is dark, grotesque, or sere, the landscape around me takes on these qualities—as sure as the nose on my face. The ground is hard, the stones are sharp, and every gnat in the area has found my eyes. If what I remember is joyful, encouraging, or empowering, the landscape around me dances and jumps, the ravens circle my head like circus performers, and the darkling beetles bumble through my camp with glee.

Sometimes, when healing needs to be done, tears come, tears of shame or guilt. More often, we wait numbly for the memory to grow into fullness. We can pass judgment on ourselves. But we know that self-condemnation will get us nowhere. In time, the punishing memory will pass, to be supplanted by other, softer memories. There have been times when we have felt absolutely crushed by the weight of negative memory-feelings. If we can wait patiently, sooner or later the negative will merge with the positive. The eyes of our lives will open wider to include the whole of who we are. We will enter a state of grace.

All the while the wilderness feels us, remembers us. We are an extension of itself.

I remember a time when I was fasting alone in the Inyo Mountains. When at the very moment I had sunk deep into the miasma of my own stupidity, a meadow lark perched on a nearby bush and sang its liquid cadence over and over again. I was so immersed in the tragedy of myself I hardly heard.

I stayed in that black hole all through the night, wrestling with nightmares and anger at others. In the morning, I awoke to bright sunshine and the unseen call of another little bird—only a little canyon wren, but surely she was an angel sent to me! Entranced, I listened to her sparse little song for hours.

What about the meadow lark? Why hadn't I been able to give her my full attention? Because I was engrossed in the act of self-healing. To this day I remember the lark as a symbol of that murky integration-land of memories I had to travel in order to become whole. And the little wren? The wren was singing that it could have been the other way around. Her song could just as well have been a dirge of mourning, and the meadow lark's a harbinger of summer.

Does natural healing last forever? No more than a full belly sustains the psyche through days of fasting. We must go back to the source over and over again, to remember those discoveries in the labyrinths of soul that lead to self-healing.

In the wilderness there is no likelihood that we will become inflated with our own importance, or consider ourselves to be forever transformed. There is nothing like a great storm to sweep away every shred of gloating ego. At such times we are not at all certain where the center of the storm lies. In ourselves? Outside ourselves? Am I projecting my own storm into the storm? Or is the storm possessing me?

I have been in storms when all I could do was grovel in the dirt like a weevil. And what groveled with me were all my grovel-memories. I prayed, yea, I prayed mightily, to be delivered of these memories. Like any wretch, I prayed to be spared. And I was spared, but not before I had been thoroughly purged of every attitude that stood in the way of grace.

Night after night I sit in profound silence in the center of my circle of purpose. All around me darkness, chill silence, and the soft harshness of my breathing.

I make little shufflings to keep warm and stay awake. The night deepens. The cold settles in like quartz dust. The stars pierce my upturned eyes with needles. I remember, I wish, I hope, I cry with longing. The cold cries too. Seeking solace, it clings even more firmly to my pores. Someday I will have to go naked into that darkness. I shiver, and try to turn away. But the cold knows. And the cold is hungry for sorrow. The cold wants to sit down to the table—now.

The only thing that saves me is what I have wrapped around my body—my underwear, my pants, my socks and shoes, my jacket, my cap, my sleeping bag—my faith that there will be another breath.

On a traditional Plains Indian vision fast, the quester lived alone on the sacred mountain without food or water, with a buffalo robe for warmth. That buffalo robe was sacred to We Who Have Gone Before.

Our old Paiute teacher taught us something very important about the spirit—that surely, if it resides in nature, in "Grandmother," as he called it—then spirit is tangible, as real as the dirt under our fingernails.

I remember him saying over and over again, "You white guys have it all wrong. The Great Creator does not live inside something. It is not something secret or hidden. It is that cottonwood, it is that bug, it is that stone." To the old man, the spiritual world was completely manifest. It didn't dwell in things. It *was* things—and it was alive.

The old man's way of perceiving spirit would be blasphemy to a Judeo-Christian theologian. It would be the "doctrinal"equivalent of saying the mundane was the profane, the material the spiritual—and by extension, that God was inside the snake-hiss that tempted Eve. That wouldn't do at all. If the sacred and profane were one, why would anyone need to be saved from the profane?

The old man's way is quite comfortable. It seems far more beneficial, personally, to consider the earth on which we live to be spirit. Not spiritual. Spirit. To hell with being saved from the body—to attain some kind of "incorruptible body." If I am spirit, then I will always be spirit. And when I die I will simply change into a purer form of what I am.

I know this when I am alone in the desert.

Now that winter is here, we are particularly aware of the fact of death. Ice has formed on our lake. The poplars and willows stand bare and stiff. Nothing can survive this cold that has not been prepared by the mind of winter to do so. I am astonished that anything under our feet can be alive. It looks so bruised and shrivelled. All the juice is gone.

I'm always saddened by the certain arrival of winter. Winter reminds me of the novels of Thomas Hardy and Jack London, where the harshness of winter plays the starring role. Survival of the fittest.

Not even the fittest survive, not in the end. We all go under. Winter is always there at the edge of the tide.

So I get angry at this dead stuff under my boot soles. It represents the savage absurdity of life. We all come to this. To this!

Then, when everything is quiet, I remember spring. The memory swells inside, surging against the shore of consciousness. This dead stuff is actually in the process of coming to life. Endure and see! The gray will change to green. The frost will melt into the earth. Overnight, tiny shoots of green!

We all come to this. All.

WHEN DARKNESS FALLS

Our summer garden isn't getting enough water. Something seems to have clogged up the irrigation pipes. We will have to shut the whole system down and purge the lines, one by one. But even if we solve that problem there will still be another bigger one. Squirrels (California grey sage squirrels) are getting into the garden. If we don't watch out, everything—the potatoes, beets, tomatoes, squash, melons, carrots, beans, cucumbers, corn—will disappear. Some morning I'll walk out there and nothing will be left.

The only solution to the squirrel problem is live-trapping. The problem with live-trapping is that it allows the squirrels to live. Nevertheless, I load the squirrel in the car and set it loose several miles from our home.

I don't think this method works particularly well. The squirrel pressure on our garden seems to have intensified. It seems to me it would take a hell of a lot of moxie to run three miles through the sage brush and open flats just to make it back to ye old tasty garden, but they do it. A squirrel I set loose three days ago in the alfalfa fields three miles away has apparently come home. I know it's the same squirrel because it still bears a rump scar, right where I whacked it with my willow cane after I caught it in the cucumbers.

Because he is diurnal, I figure old Scar Rump travelled this infinite distance by either day or night—or both. Since the last few days have had 150° ground temperature, I assume he covered most open terrain at night. When I count up all the nocturnal predators who would willingly dine on squirrel, I am amazed at his feat. Coyote, fox, rattlesnake, king snake, gopher snake, mountain lion, bobcat, owl . . . Once summertime darkness falls out here in the eastern Sierra, there's hell to pay.

I wonder if my migratory path will be anything like Scar Rump's. Night will fall and I'll head home from that distant clime to which my life has carried me. Who knows what fate awaits me along the way? All-too-familiar monsters of karma will be lurking behind every bush. Tail in the air, I'll run like I've never run before.

Are you all alone and hungry on the sacred mountain, watching the evening shadows yearn toward the east? Are you longing for home, for a warm kitchen and a soft bed? Are you feeling sorry for yourself? Do you wonder if you will make it through the night?

Console yourself with the thought that we are with you. There isn't a single living organism, including We Who Have Gone Before, who isn't hungry and alone, watching the night fall on the mountain of the most high.

I have never been frightened when darkness fell. I welcomed it with an open heart. I do not think one could find anything more beautiful than the appearance of stars in the sky, or the rising of the full moon on the eastern horizon. Yet when I came close to dying, I did not want to be left alone in a dark room.

I will try to rise and go into the next room, where lights are burning with the promise of life. I may even try to go toward that in-eluctable delight, but will be unable to rise. What then? Will the stars come out, one by one? Will the familiar constellations appear? Will my eyes follow the outlines of the Great Bear to the North Star? Or will I close them against the oncoming night and wish I'd never been born?

Sometimes it seems everybody has an opinion about "where I am going"—everybody but me. The closer I get, the less I seem to know. All I know for certain is that darkness will fall. And then the stars will appear.

❖❖❖❖

Those fasting grounds where, alone and hungry, I sat in the dirt and waited for night to come—there must be close to a hundred. With perfect ease I can travel back to these "present" places glinting like flakes of obsidian in the dust of noon: the Tiltil Valley; the South Warner Wilderness; the Roberts Range; the Ruby Mountains; the Eureka Valley sand dunes; the desert pavement; Forgotten Spring; Soldier Pass; Cerro Colorado Sur; Providence Mountains; Reese River; Robinson Hole; Joshua Flats; Paiute Canyon; DeDeckera Canyon; Papoose Flat; Navarro River; Coon Bay; Black Mountains; Spook Canyon; Taboose Creek; Crater Mountain; Addie Canyon; Andrew's Mountain; Black Spring; Crooked Creek; Robert's Ridge; Wyman Creek; Whippoorwill Flat; McMurray's Meadow; Queen of Sheba; Funeral Peak; Jubilee Pass; Indian Pass; Red Wall Canyon; Hunter Mountain; Grapevine Creek; Bighorn Gorge; Forgotten Creek; Last Chance Range; Eureka Valley; Cottonwood Canyon; Death Valley Buttes; Mormon Point; Death Valley Wash; Confidence Hills; Shoreline Butte; Keane Spring; Lemoigne Canyon; Saline Range . . . .

Mainly, I remember the places in Death Valley, my wilderness home. So many ashes of former bodies have been scattered there. I have grovelled in the dirt, tunneled like a sewer rat, shed tears into stony ground, blistered in the unforgiving sun, screamed into the thick-empty darkness—of Death Valley. When I finally die for good, I will go to that great *graben* in the earth, that sink hole of salt, where water is but a rumor on the wind. I will lay me down beneath a creosote bush and wait for the coming of night.

To those who fast on the sacred mountain waiting for dawn: Do not be afraid to be afraid. Be afraid, exult, hope, despair, wait, and wonder.

And then love.

> If the wind means me,
> I'm here!
> Here.

—Theodore Roethke

Selene Foster: Mixed media on paper, '99